The Formac Pocketguide to

Nova Scotia
Birds

120 Common Inland Birds

Written & illustrated by Jeffrey C. Domm

Formac Publishing Company Limited
Halifax, Nova Scotia

Formac Publishing Company Limited acknowledges the support of the Cultural Affairs Section, Nova Scotia Department of Tourism and Culture. We acknowledge the financial support of the Government of Canada through the Book Publishing Industry Development Program (BPIDP) for our publishing activities. We acknowledge the support of the Canada Council for the Arts for our publishing program.

Canadian Cataloguing in Publication Data

Domm, Jeff, 1958-
      Formac pocketguide to Nova Scotia Birds
      (Formac pocketguide)

      Includes index.
      ISBN 0-88780-507-8

1. Birds -- Nova Scotia -- Identification.   2. Bird watching -- Nova Scotia -- Guidebooks.   I. Title.   II. Title: Pocketguide to Nova Scotia birds.   III. Series.

QL685.5.N6D65 2000   598'.09716   C00-950155-X

For my parents, Bob and Mary Lou Domm, who always supported me in my artistic endeavors. And to all those people who are striving to protect the remaining bird habitats in Nova Scotia.
Jeffrey C. Domm

I would like to acknowledge the help of the entire staff at Formac Publishing for their support and input into the production of this book.

Cartography by Peggy McCalla

Formac Publishing Company Limited
5502 Atlantic Street
Halifax, Nova Scotia
Canada B3H 1G4

Printed and bound in Canada

Contents

Introduction	4	Larks	60
How to Use This Guide	5	Longspurs	61
		Meadowlarks	62
Nova Scotia Birding Hot Spots	6	Martins	63
		Nighthawks	64
Blackbirds	12	Nuthatches	65
Buntings	17	Ospreys	67
Cardinals	18	Owls	68
Chickadees	19	Peewees	72
Creepers	21	Pheasants	73
Crossbills	22	Phoebes	74
Crows	24	Ravens	75
Doves	25	Shrikes	76
Eagles	27	Siskins	77
Falcons	28	Sparrows	78
Finches	30	Swallows	87
Flycatchers	33	Swifts	91
Grosbeaks	38	Tanagers	92
Grouse	41	Thrushes	93
Hawks	44	Vireos	97
Hummingbirds	51	Warblers	100
Jays	52	Waxwings	119
Juncos	54	Whip-poor-wills	120
Kestrels	55	Woodcocks	121
Kingbirds	56	Woodpeckers	122
Kingfishers	57	Wrens	127
Kinglets	58	Index	128

Introduction

Nova Scotia is a rich landscape of forest, meadow, river, lake, marsh, beach and ocean. Situated on the migration path of the Atlantic flyway, it is an excellent place to observe birds on their seasonal journey between their breeding and wintering grounds. In summer and fall, more than 300 species can be identified around the province, many of them in full mating plumage. In winter, a variety of birds can be seen at backyard feeders as well as in the wild, especially on calm, mild days.

When observing birds in the wild it isn't always easy to make a correct identification, especially if the birds are a great distance away, and there are obstacles, such as foliage, in your way. The visual keys in this book will help you quickly compare the information about each bird with the living specimen.

The illustrations have been painted specially for this book. They are drawn from several sources, including photographs, observations, scientific specimens and written descriptions. They emphasize the key features — shape, colour, markings and size. Each one represents a typical specimen: it is helpful to remember that plumage variations are to be expected and that colours change in different light conditions.

Along with each full-colour illustration, there are diagrams that depict the nesting locations, egg sizes and colour, backyard-feeder preferences, and seasonal range. Descriptions of the birds' distinctive markings and their calls and songs also help identify birds, both perched and in flight.

The 120 birds were selected from the more than 400 possible species which have been observed in Nova Scotia. Many of them are birds you can expect to see anywhere in the province; others have more limited range and are found in only specific areas. The contents are arranged in alphabetical order of genus names, found on the top of each page. The species are alphabetical within each genus group.

Before setting out on a birdwatching trip in Nova Scotia, be sure to dress warmly and watch the weather. Storms can move in quickly over the ocean and bring high winds and cold temperatures, even in summer. These changes can affect the number of birds you see, not to mention dampening your spirits.

Nova Scotia is fortunate in still having areas of untouched habitats favoured by birds. However, the threat of human contact is increasing daily. Only two percent of Nova Scotia beaches are formally restricted from building; there are no clear-cutting laws in effect in the woods; industrial waste is evident in water and on land; and the protection of endangered species is far behind that of other countries. Birds of all sizes play an important role in the balance of nature. Their place in the food chain has been severely disrupted by desertification, deforestation and by the widespread use of pesticides in agriculture. With this guide you can readily appreciate the abundant variety of bird life and come to know by name and by call many of the birds of eastern North America.

How to use this guide

Birds don't stay in one place for very long, so it is important to learn a few simple rules to help you quickly identify them. Most often what you see is a bird that is feeding; perhaps it is hopping along the ground or flitting from branch to branch. Maybe it is perched in a tree, preparing to fly away at any second. The visual keys given in this guide focus in on the primary identifiable features of each bird, namely, colour, outline and size. The secondary features are the habitat, the colour details and variations, given in the text, the egg size and colour, and the shape of the feet.

When you are looking at a bird, first estimate the size, then take note of the shape of the wings, tail, head, beak and feet. Note any particular marks — patches, streaks, stripes and speckles. Watch its movements to see how it flies, hops and feeds.

Legend for visual keys

1 **Size identification** — the rectangle represents the page of this book, and the silhouette of the bird represents its size against this page.

2 **Foot type** — (a) Anisodactyl (b) Zygodactyl

3 **Egg** — actual size and shape unless otherwise indicated.

4 **Backyard feeder** — there are three types of bird feeders to which small birds might be attracted.

5 **Birdhouse nester** — some species are happy to make their nest in a manmade house which you might hang in your garden.

6 **Nesting location**

▼ Hollow in ground   ▼ Waterside plants
▽ Bushes and thickets   ▼ Cavities of trees
▽ Deciduous trees   ▼ Conifers and tall
▼ Tall, dead, decaying trees   trees
▽ Banks along rivers and ponds
▽ Cliffs and/or rocky ledges

7 **Observation calendar** — the bar gives the initial for each of the twelve months of the year. The deeper colour indicates the best months for seeing the species, according to known migration patterns.

Observation Calendar
J F M A M J J A S O N D

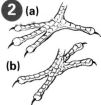

Nova Scotia Birding
HOT SPOTS

Evangeline Trail

1 **Uniacke Estate Museum Park** This 2125-hectare (5000-acre) estate offers a range of walking trails in old growth forests, meadows and around the lakeshore. A wide variety of warblers and other small songbirds, as well as hawks, can be seen here. On Highway 101 follow the signs for Mount Uniacke and the park.

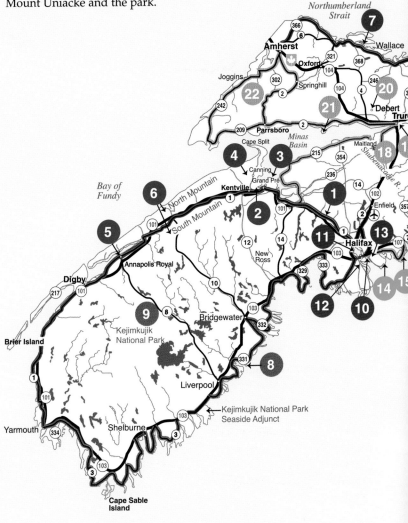

SCENIC TRAILS

- Cabot Trail
- Evangeline Trail
- Fleur-de-lys Trail
- Glooscap Trail
- Halifax and Dartmouth
- Lighthouse Route
- Marconi Trail
- Marine Drive
- Sunrise Trail

CAPE BRETON ISLAND

Atlantic Ocean

3 Evangeline Beach Although the majority of spottings that take place here are waterfowl, it is also possible to see birds of prey pursuing migrating birds. Best times for birdwatching are spring and fall.

2 Wolfville At the Robie Tufts Nature Centre one can see Chimney Swifts gather throughout the summer, as well as find information about birding places in the Wolfville area. There are opportunities to spot Merlins here: they have been known to nest right in the town. You may see them chasing swallows.

4 **Sheffield Mills** Several years ago a farmer decided to throw some food out for Bald Eagles that visited the area during the winter months. The result was that Sheffield Mills is perhaps the best place in central and south Nova Scotia for seeing these large birds of prey, winter and summer. There are now nesting birds in the area, along with Red-tailed Hawks, Rough-legged Hawks, ravens and crows. Some of the best interaction between eagles and ravens can be observed here. Take Highway 101 to exit 11, and continue on to Canning. Signs with eagle symbols lead you to Sheffield Mills.

5 **Annapolis Royal Historic Gardens** In the centre of Annapolis Royal there is a beautiful public garden. With all the blossoms in summer you are sure to see Ruby-throated Hummingbirds dart across your path, as well as many songbirds and other small birds. On the backside of the garden is a marsh which attracts Red-winged Blackbirds and hawks.

6 **South and North Mountains** March and April are courting months in the South and North Mountains of the Annapolis Valley. Several species of owls have been encouraged by the construction of nesting boxes. If you are good at imitating owl hoots, you may be rewarded with an answer. Northern Harriers and Red-tailed Hawks are found nesting in the region as well on the Canard and Grand Pré dykes.

Sunrise Trail

7 **Wallace Bay Wildlife Area** The marsh at the head of Wallace Bay is preserved by Ducks Unlimited and the Canadian Wildlife Service. The trail, on a raised portion of a dyke, offers an opportunity to see many marsh birds, including Red-winged Blackbirds and many species of song birds. Also in the Wallace area, at the mouth of the Wallace River, one can see Kingfishers, Northern Harriers, Kestrels and Bald Eagles.

Lighthouse Route

8 **Cherry Hill Beach** This South Shore beach, near Bridgewater, is an excellent location to see inland birds that enjoy marshland. There is a boardwalk takes you around the marsh as well as a very beautiful beach.

9 **Kejimkujik National Park** The woodland trails in Keji are excellent for birdwatching, indeed, some of the best in the province for seeing and hearing a wide variety of inland birds, including warblers, finches, flycatchers, and woodpeckers. In addition there are larger birds — hawks, eagles, and Ospreys. The park is on Route 8, between Liverpool and Annapolis Royal.

Halifax Regional Municipality

0 McNabs Island At the entrance to Halifax Harbour is a large island that makes for an excellent day-trip from the city. There are hiking trails leading to old forts and secluded beaches. The island is home to Ospreys, as well as a wide variety of warblers, finches and flycatchers.

1 Hemlock Ravine A few minutes from downtown Halifax, very close to the shores of Bedford Basin, is the woodland park called Hemlock Ravine, once part of a large estate owned by Sir John Wentworth. The paths meander through mixed woodland, which is home to chickadees, nuthatches, juncos, warblers and Ruffed Grouse.

2 Long Lake Park Reserve Once part of the watershed for Halifax, this 6000-acre park has many trails, including the old coach road to St Margaret's Bay, now a track enjoyed by mountain bikers. With its several lakes, and variety of habitats, including marsh and old farm land, many species of inland birds, including finches, warblers, thrushes and occasional owls can be seen and heard here. Take St. Margaret's Bay Road from the Armdale Rotary for 2 km to a parking area just before the turn-off to Peggys Cove.

3 Trans Canada Trail Recycling the old rail beds into trails has brought into being a route across marshes, through wooded areas and close to sandy beaches in the Cole Harbour area. As part of the Trans Canada trail, this is a treat for bird-watchers. The parking area is off Bissett Road in Cole Harbour.

Marine Drive

14 Conrad Beach Twenty minutes from Dartmouth, taking route 207 towards Lawrencetown, you will see a sign on the right for Conrad Road. Follow this to the parking area behind the dunes. On either side is a broad marsh where many small inland birds can be seen.

15 Three Fathom Harbour and Grand Desert On route 207 from Dartmouth, you will pass through Lawrencetown Beach before coming to Three Fathom Harbour. As you make your way down to Fishermen's Reserve you will pass a marsh on the left where there are excellent viewing opportunities for flycatchers, warblers, sparrows and hawks. Further along route 207, at Grand Desert, take Dyke Road. Park at the end and go right to find an old shooting range, with dunes, or left to ascend a wooded hill and look out over the marshes. From the top you have an excellent view of the area and can see Bobolinks, nuthatches, and Boreal Chickadees, as well as many other common species.

16 **Martinique Beach** From Musquodoboit Harbour follow the signs to Martinique Beach, an exceptionally long stretch of typical marsh-dune-beach landscape. Around the marsh you can see hawks, warblers, finches, and flycatchers, as well as the occasional bird of prey.

17 **Taylors Head Provincial Park** Drive east on route 7 towards Sheet Harbour. The park is well signposted after Lake Charlotte.The figure-eight trail from the parking lot out to the headland goes through a variety of habitats — marsh, sandy beach, rocky shoreline, softwood forest, barrens and abandoned farmland. Many of the common inland birds can be seen in this hikers' paradise.

Glooscap Trail

18 **Shubenacadie River** There are many sites along the Shubenacadie River where one can see Bald Eagles. Route 2 from Enfield and Route 215 from Shubenacadie follow the river quite closely. Alternatively one can take a boat trip to see the nesting sites on the cliffs at the lower end of the river.

19 **Victoria Park** In Truro take Willow Street to this mixed-forest area, home to many year-round inhabitants, including chickadees, jays, woodpeckers, kinglets, thrushes, warblers and several species of hawks and owls.

20 **Debert Game Sanctuary/McElmon's Pond** The variety of habitats found in this location offers some great birdwatching. Songbirds of many kinds nest here, including Cedar Waxwings, Eastern Wood-pewees, kinglets, vireos and warblers. With all this activity you are also bound to see a few hawks. Take Trans Canada Highway to Debert (exit 13) and watch for signs and a picnic park.

21 **Economy Mountain Trail** This mixed-forest area is excellent for viewing Gray Jays, Northern Parula, Black-throated Green Warblers, Boreal Chickadees, Black-backed Woodpeckers and Ruffed Grouse. The trail is within Five Islands Provincial Park on Highway 2.

22 **Chignecto Game Sanctuary** This wonderful wildlife sanctuary is a great place to spot grosbeaks, Gray Jays, White-winged Crossbills, Northern Goshawks, Pileated Woodpeckers and a variety of songbirds. Take highway 2 out of Parrsboro for 12 km, to the Boars Back Road which leads though the sanctuary.

Marconi Trail

23 **Cape Perce** East of Donkin, on the trail that leads to Port Morien, look for an unpaved road, just past Schooner Pond Cove. The track leads to an abandoned mine where you can park. On your right there is a marsh that is home to a wide variety of birds. In the other direction there are woods and finally, an open headland. This is one of the best places in Cape Breton to view birds in various habitats.

Cabot Trail

24 **Cape Breton Highlands National Park** There are many hiking trails in the park that provide excellent birdwatching. In the forests, such as on the Lone Sheiling Trail, you will see and hear many of songbirds. In the barrens and evergreen forests, such as on the Benjies Lake Trail, you may come across an owl in the evening, and in the day, warblers and Cedar Waxwings. The Lake of Islands Trail goes deep into the highlands, through hardwoods, softwoods and finally out into the barrens. Information on the trails can be obtained at the entrance to the park.

Fleur-de-lys Trail

25 **Big Pond** Route 4, between Sydney and St. Peters, runs along the lake, giving some spectacular views and the opportunity to see Bald Eagles. At Big Pond there are organized nature tours to see the breeding grounds.

Bobolink

Dolichonyx oryzivorus

Observation Calendar

J F M A M J J A S O N D

Male: *Summer:* Black overall with pale yellow patch on back of head; back black changing to large white patch down to rump; wings have white patches and edges; feet, legs, and bill black. In flight: White rump is revealed. Tail has sharp pointed feathers.
Female and **male** *(winter)*: brown and buff overall with black streaks over top of head; legs red.

Did you know? These birds need hayfield habitat to survive. Studies show that most young will die when farmers' fields are mown before they have a chance to fledge.

Voice: Song is a light phrase that increases in pitch and has been described as *Bob o link - bob o link spink spank spink.* Usually sings in flight. Call is metallic *clink.*
Nest/eggs: Slight hollow in ground with bulky gathering of grass and weed stalks. Lined with fine grass in areas near water and within waterside plants. 4-7 eggs.
Food: A variety of insects and weed seeds.

Brown-headed Cowbird

Molothrus ater

Foot: Anisodactyl

Egg: Actual Size

Observation Calendar

J F M A M J J A S O N D

Male: Brown head, glossy black overall; feet and legs black; sharp black bill.

Female: Overall grey with dark brown wings and tail; faint buff streaking on chest down to lower belly, feet and legs are black.

Did you know? Molothrus ater, the Cowbird's scientific name, means dark, greedy beggar, an apt name for a bird that leaves its eggs for other birds to hatch.

Voice: A squeaky *weee titi.*

Nest/eggs: Parasite. Builds no nest. 1 egg.

Food: A variety of insects, weed seeds, grain and grass.

Nesting Location

Common Grackle
Quiscalus quiscula

Observation Calendar

J F M A M J J A S O N D

Male: Overall iridescent black and purple; bright yellow eye; black bill long and sharp; feet and legs are charcoal grey; long tail.

Female: Similar but duller iridescent colouring, tail is shorter.

Did you know? Flocks in the thousands gather on fields and cause a lot of damage to farmers' crops.

Voice: Chatter is a metallic and rasping *grideleeeeek*. Calls are *chak chah*.

Food: A variety of ground insects, seeds, grain, minnows, rodents and crayfish.

Nest/eggs: Loose bulky cup built with weed stalks, twigs, grass, debris, lined with feather and grass, in conifer tree or shrubs. Will occasionally use an osprey's nest. Prefers to nest in colonies. 3-6 eggs.

European Starling
Sturnus vulgaris

Size Identification

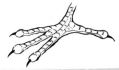

Foot: Anisodactyl

Egg: Actual Size

Observation Calendar
J F M A M J J A S O N D

Male/Female: *Summer:* Black iridescent bird in summer with light white speckles over entire body; bill is sharp yellow; wing and tail are edged in white and brown; feet and legs are red. *Winter:* Speckles increase and some become brown; bill is black; feet and legs are red; wings and tail have more brown.

Did you know? Sixty starlings were introduced into New York City in 1890. Since then they have spread throughout North America.

Backyard Feeder

Voice: Mimics the songs of other birds and even sounds of cats and whistles.
Food: A variety of insects including worms and grubs and weed seeds.
Nest/eggs: Loose cup in cavity filled with grass, leaves, cloth and feathers, up to 18 metres above the ground. 4-5 eggs.

Birdhouse Nester

Nesting Location

Red-winged Blackbird
Agelaius phoeniceus

Size Identification

Foot: Anisodactyl

Egg: Actual Size

Backyard Feeder

Observation Calendar

J F M A M J J A S O N D

Male: Black overall with distinctive red shoulder patch bordered with light yellow at bottom.
Female: Brown with buff eyebrows and chin; chest and belly buff streaked with dark brown; wings and tail feathers brown with buff edges.

Did you know? Red-winged Blackbirds are prolific breeders, sometimes breeding three times in one season. They are seen in freshwater marshes throughout the province.

Voice: Song is *ocaaleee ocaalee*.
Food: A variety of insects and weed seeds.
Nest/eggs: Bulky cup built of leaves, rushes, grass, rootlets, moss and milkweed fibre, lined with grass, in tall waterside plants near water. 3-4 eggs.

Nesting Location

Snow Bunting
Plectrophenax nivalis

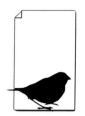

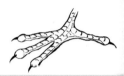

Observation Calendar

J F M A M J J A S O N D

Male: *Summer*: White overall with black wings and tail; tail has white edges; wings have large white patches on shoulder and flight feathers; feet and legs black; black bill, short and sharp. In flight: wings white.
Female and male in *winter* have brown and rust blotches.

Did you know? Accustomed to cold and heavy snowfall, the Snow Bunting will dig a hole in the snow to escape from a storm.

Voice: Song is a chorus of whistles. Call includes *buzzy tew*.
Food: A variety of insects, tree buds and seeds.
Nest/eggs: Cup, low to ground, in tree or shrub. 3-5 eggs.
(NB Does not nest in Nova Scotia.)

Northern Cardinal

Cardinalis cardinalis

Size Identification

Foot: Anisodactyl

Egg: Actual Size

Backyard Feeder

Observation Calendar
J F M A M J J A S O N D

Male: Brilliant red overall with a stout red-orange bill, crested head; black mask beginning at base of bill resembling a small bib; feet dark red.
Female: Buff and grey with hints of bright red on crest, wings and back. Stout red-orange bill with black mask beginning at base of bill (bib may appear smaller), feet are dark red.

Did you know? The cardinal gets its name from its bright red colour which resembles that of the robes and hat of a Roman Catholic cardinal.

Breeds in southwestern regions of the province and is extending its range.

Voice: Song is a series of repeated whistles *wheit wheit wheit, cheer cheer cheer.* Also *chip.*
Food: Seeds, fruits, grains and various insects.
Nest/eggs: Woven cup of twigs, vines, leaves and grass, 2-3 metres above ground, in dense shrubbery. 2-5 eggs.

Nesting Location

Black-capped Chickadee

Poecile atricapilla

Size Identification

Size Identification

Foot: Anisodactyl

Observation Calendar

J F M A M J J A S O N D

Male/Female: Round black head with white cheeks; black chin that contrasts against bright white bib which fades into rust on belly with buff edges; wings black and grey with white edges; tail black with white edges; feet and legs black.

Did you know? In winter Black-capped Chickadees form small flocks of about 10 birds and defend their territory from intruders.

Voice: A descending whistle with two notes and sounds like *chick-a-dee-dee-dee*.
Food: Seeds, insects and berries. Drawn to thistle-seed feeders.
Nest/eggs: Domed cup lined with wool, hair, fur, moss and insect cocoons, in cavity of tree. 5-10 eggs.

Egg: Actual Size

Backyard Feeder

Birdhouse Nester

Nesting Location

Boreal Chickadee
Poecile hudsonica

Observation Calendar

J F M A M J J A S O N D

Male/Female: Dirty brown cap with white cheeks; black chin contrasted against white belly with rust colour sides; back brown; wings and tail charcoal with white edges and black tips; feet and legs charcoal.

Did you know? During winter months they will forage for food with Black-capped Chickadees searching for hibernating insects and insect eggs.

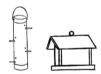

Seen in interior of the province, in woodland areas.

Voice: Song is slow *chick che day day day* with calls that are distinctive chip.
Food: Insects, insect eggs, seeds.
Nest/eggs: Domed nest lined with fur, hair, plant down, moss and feathers in cavity of tree or dug in decaying stump. 4-9 eggs.

Brown Creeper
Certhia americana

Observation Calendar

J F M A M J J A S O N D

Male/Female: Overall brown with grey streaks and white chin, chest and belly; long curved bill that is black on top and white/pink on bottom; distinctive eye stripe; feet and legs grey; tail is long and pointed.

Egg: Actual Size

Did you know? Spending most of its day creeping up and down trees looking for meals, the Brown Creeper can flatten itself and blend into the colour of the tree trunk when a predator passes by.

Backyard Feeder

Voice: A very high whistling *see wee see tu eee.*
Food: Insects, insect and spider eggs and occasionally nuts and seeds.
Nest/eggs: Cup with foundation of twig, bark, and leaves, lined with bark, grass, feathers and moss, in cavity or under loose bark of tree, up to 5 metres above ground. 4-8 eggs.

Nesting Location

Red Crossbill

Loxia curvirostra

Size Identification

Foot: Anisodactyl

Egg: Actual Size

Backyard Feeder

Observation Calendar

J F M A M J J A S O N D

Male: Brick red overall with brightest area on rump; wings and tail dull brown with white edges; back brick red with dull grey banding; grey bill is crossed over at the end.
Female: Similar to male except grey overall with varying amounts of olive on head and back, yellow chest with slight brown banding, rump is yellow.

Did you know? Listen for the cracking of cones when searching for the Crossbill. They can be found snipping off branches with cones on them.

Not very common. Seen near Annapolis Royal and Mount Uniacke Estate.

Voice: Call is *Chipa chipa chipa, che che che che.*
Food: Conifer seeds, variety of insects and other seeds.
Nest/eggs: Bulky cup built with twig, rootlets, and bark, lined with feathers, grass and fur, in conifers, well away from trunk, in a thicket of needles. 3-5 eggs.

Nesting Location

White-winged Crossbill

Loxia leucoptera

Size Identification

Foot: Anisodactyl

Male: Overall pinkish-red with long black bill that crosses over at the end; wings and tail black, with two large white bars; lower belly turns grey; feet and legs charcoal.
Female: Similar to male except greyish with olive areas on back and head, yellow on chest and rump.

Egg: Actual Size

Did you know? Their bills are used to scrap conifer seeds by forcing open the cone and pulling seeds out.

Appear in large numbers in wooded areas near the shore.

Backyard Feeder

Voice: Call to each other *peeet* with a flight call of *chif chif*.
Food: Conifer seeds, variety of insects and other seeds.
Nest/eggs: Deep cup built with twig, small roots, weed stalks, moss, lichen, and bark, lined with grass, feather and hair, in spruce tree or shrub, 2-3 metres above ground. 2-5 egg.

Nesting Location

American Crow

Corvus brachyrhynchos

Observation Calendar

J F M A M J J A S O N D

Male/Female: Overall shiny black with a hint of purple in direct sunlight; large broad black bill; short and slightly square tail; feet and legs black.

Did you know? Although one might think that crows are a nuisance bird, they actually devour large quantities of grasshoppers, beetles and grubs that can be destructive to crops.

Voice: A variety of calls. Most common is the long *caaaaaw* which softens at the end.
Food: Omnivorous – insects, food waste, grains, seeds and carrion.
Nest/eggs: Large basket of twigs, sticks, vines, moss, feathers, fur and hair, on ledge in crotch of tree or shrub. 3-4 eggs.

Mourning Dove

Zenaida macroura

Size Identification

Foot: Anisodactyl

Egg: Actual Size

Observation Calendar
J F M A M J J A S O N D

Male: Buff coloured head and body; dark grey wings and tail; bill is black with speckles of red at opening; wings have small black feathers highlighted against softer grey, eyes black surrounded by light blue; feet and legs red; tail is long and pointed.

Female: Similar except for head, neck and chest are evenly brown.

Did you know? When the mourning dove is in flight its wings whistle.

Backyard Feeder

Voice: Very distinct cooing sound that sounds a little sad, *coooahooo oo oo oo* fading at the end.

Food: A variety of seeds and grain

Nest/eggs: Platform of sticks and twigs, lined with grass and rootlets, in evergreens, 15 metres above ground. 1-2 eggs.

Nesting Location

Rock Dove (Pigeon)
Columba livia

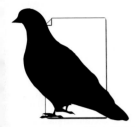

Foot: Anisodactyl

Egg: Actual Size

Backyard Feeder

Observation Calendar

J F M A M J J A S O N D

Male/Female: Varies greatly from solid white to solid black and everything in between. Most birds have dark grey head with hints of iridescent colours along the neck; body light grey with two charcoal wing bands; tail and wings dark grey with black bands; rump is white.

Did you know? Pigeons were introduced to North America in the 1800s. They are now prevalent everywhere, especially in urban areas.

Voice: Soft descending *kooooo kooooo*.
Food: Seeds and grain
Nest/eggs: Flimsy nest of twigs, grass, straw and debris, on ledges or crevices of buildings and bridges, in colonies. 1-2 eggs.

Nesting Location

Bald Eagle
Haliaeetus leucocephalus

Size Identification

Foot: Anisodactyl

Observation Calendar
J F M A M J J A S O N D

Egg: 75%

Male/Female: In flight: Broad black wings and belly with white head and tail feathers. Perched: White head with brilliant yellow eyes, white tail feathers, black back and wings, feet and legs yellow; bill yellow.
Juvenile: Mistaken for Golden Eagle because it lacks white head and tail; chest, white and speckled; black wings with white speckles; underparts black with large areas of white.

Did you know? The eagle population is now recovering from rapid declines in the 1970s due to the widespread use of DDT.

Large numbers are seen at Sheffield Mills in winter. In summer they can be seen in Cape Breton.

Voice: A loud scream given in multiples.
Food: A variety of small and medium-sized mammals, fish and carrion.
Nest/eggs: Upper parts of large, often dead, trees built with large twigs, lined with grass, moss, sod and weeds. 2 eggs.

Nesting Location

Merlin

Falco columbarius

Observation Calendar

J F M A M J J A S O N D

Male: In flight: Buff underside with dark brown banding overall; dark brown head with thin buff eyebrow; tail dark. Perched: Slate-blue wings with slight amount of white edges; bill black with yellow at base; feet and legs pale yellow.
Female: Brown back and wings; buff underparts with brown streaks.

Did you know? Often called the "bullet hawk," this is a very fast bird when racing after its prey. It has a wonderful ability to turn quickly and accelerate in flight, even through thick woods.

Voice: Rapid and high-pitched *clee clee clee.*
Food: Small birds in flight, reptiles, amphibians and insects.
Nest/eggs: Stick interwoven with moss, twigs, lichen and conifer needles, on cliff ledge or cavity of tree. 4-5 eggs.

Peregrine Falcon
Falco peregrinus

Observation Calendar
J F M A M J J A S O N D

Male/Female: In flight: Overall white underside with charcoal banding; face has black mask and sideburns with yellow around dark eyes, bill is yellow and grey, feet and legs are yellow. Perched: Black wings with buff edging on feathers.

Egg: 70%

Did you know? The Peregrine can reach the fastest speeds of any animal on earth — 260 km/h.

Seen only in southwestern coastal regions where breeding pairs were reintroduced in recent years.

Voice: A series of high pitched screams *ki ki ki.*
Food: Catches birds in flight and occasionally will eat larger insects.
Nest/eggs: Slight hollow in rock ledge or flat roof top, built with sticks. 3-5 eggs.

American Goldfinch

Carduelis tristis

Size Identification

Foot: Anisodactyl

Egg: Actual Size

Backyard Feeder

Observation Calendar
J F M A M J J A S O N D

Male: *Summer:* Bright yellow overall with black forehead and yellow bill; black wings with white bands; tail black with white edges; rump white; feet and legs red. *Winter:* Similar yellow is replaced by gray with hints of yellow.
Female and **male** *(winter)*: similar except overall grey/brown with yellow highlights.

Voice: Sing as they fly with a succession of chips and twitters, *per chic o ree per chic o ree.*
Food: A variety of insects but mostly interested in thistle and weed seeds.
Nest/eggs: Neat cup built with fibres woven together, lined with thistle and feather down, in leafy tree or shrubs in upright branches, 1-5 metres above ground. 4-6 eggs.

Nesting Location

Purple Finch

Carpodacus purpureus

Observation Calendar

J F M A M J J A S O N D

Male: Red upper parts with black banding on back; rump is red; chest is red with white feathers banding down to lower belly which is all white; wings and tail are black with white edges; bill is broad and yellow; feet and legs grey.
Female: Brown with white eyebrow and brown eyeline; chest white with brown streaks down front; wings and tail dull brown with white edges; feet and legs grey.

Voice: Song is long and musical ending in downward trill. Call *chirp.*
Food: A variety of insects, berries, weed seeds, and buds of trees.
Nest/eggs: Shallow cup built with twig, grass, bark strip and small roots, lined with grass and hair, in evergreen tree or shrub, 5-60 feet above ground. 3-5 eggs.

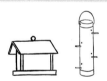

House Finch

Carpodacus mexicanus

Observation Calendar

J F M A M J J A S O N D

Male: Red crown, chin and chest which changes to buff at belly; wings and tail brown, feet and legs grey, grey bill, white undertail, dark brown banding around the sides.
Female: All greyish brown with faint banding down sides.

These are fairly new arrivals and have recently begun establishing breeding grounds in southern regions of the province.

Voice: Musical warble ending with *jeeeeer*.
Food: Weed seeds, fruit, buds.
Nest/eggs: Cup of lined weed and grass, roots, feathers, string and twigs, 1-2 metres above ground. 4-5 eggs.

32

Alder Flycatcher

Empidonax alnorum

Size Identification

Foot: Anisodactyl

Male/Female: Dark olive/brown from head down back; wings and tail feathers black and olive green with white wing bars; throat white with a pale yellow belly; eye is black surrounded by very light yellow ring; feet and legs are charcoal.

Egg: Actual Size

Voice: The call is a simple *peeeep* while the song is *rreeeebeeet* or *rreeebeeaa* with the accent on the second syllable.
Food: Flying insects.
Nest/eggs: Loose cup built with grass, moss, bark, twigs, and silky items with plant strips dangling in upright fork of tree or shrub, within 2 metres above ground. 3-4 eggs.

Nesting Location

Great Crested Flycatcher

Myiarchus crinitus

Size Identification

Foot: Anisodactyl

Egg: Actual Size

Observation Calendar

J F M A M J J A S O N D

Male/Female: Olive/grey head with crest; back is olive/grey; wings are black with olive/grey edges and rust colour on outer edge; tail strong reddish-brown; throat soft grey changing to pale yellow at belly; feet and legs black.

Did you know? The Great Crested Flycatcher will sometimes use foil or cellophane in its nest because it is attracted to reflective objects.

Voice: A throaty whistle *wheeep* or a rolling *prrrreeeet*.
Food: Flying insects and a variety of ground insects.
Nest/eggs: Bulky cup built with twig, leaves, feather, bark and cast off snakeskin, or cellophane, in natural cavity of tree, up to 18 metres above ground. 4-8 eggs.

Birdhouse Nester

Nesting Location

34

Least Flycatcher

Empidonax minimus

Observation Calendar

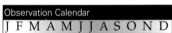

J F M A M J J A S O N D

Male/Female: Smallest of the flycatchers with a brown/olive head and back; rump is slightly golden; throat white and washes to a grey breast and a pale yellow belly; black eye is ringed with white; wings dark brown and black with white wing bands; tail dark olive/brown with white edges.

Did you know? The Least Flycatcher is not afraid of humans and in pursuit of a flying insect will dive within inches of a person.

Voice: Song is *chibic chibic chibic* repeated with accent in middle of phrase.
Food: Flying insects.
Nest/eggs: Compact and deep cup built with bark, weeds, grasses and lined with thistle, feathers, hair and fibres, in upright fork of tree or shrub, 1-20 metres above ground. 3-6 eggs.

Olive-sided Flycatcher

Contopus cooperi

Size Identification

Foot: Anisodactyl

Egg: Actual Size

Observation Calendar
J F M A M J J A S O N D

Male/Female: Dark grey/olive overall with crest at back of head; bar of white that runs down front from under chin to lower belly; white tufts on sides of rump but could be hidden by wings; feet and legs black; bill black on top with yellow underside.

Voice: a loud whistled hick, *three-bee-er* with first word quieter then others and the second is accented. A warning *chirp pip pip pip*.

Food: Flying insects.

Nest/eggs: Flat cup attached to horizontal branch of conifer tree or shrub built with twigs, small roots and lichens and lined with pine needles and small roots, 2-15 metres above ground. 3 eggs.

Nesting Location

36

Yellow-bellied Flycatcher

Empidonax flaviventris

Observation Calendar

J F M A M J J A S O N D

Male: Olive green head, back, wings and tail feathers; yellowish throat and breast; wings have two yellow bands; black eye has yellow ring; feet and legs black; thin bill is dark grey on top with yellow underside or it can be all dark.

Voice: A simple and sweet *pu-wee peawee*.
Food: Flying insects.
Nest/eggs: Deep cup built with mosses and lined with black rootlets, pine needles, grass and moss, on or near ground, at base of conifer tree. 3-4 eggs.

Evening Grosbeak

Coccothraustes vespertinus

Observation Calendar

J F M A M J J A S O N D

Male: Dark brown/black head with dull yellow stripe across forehead that blends into a dull yellow at the shoulders; tail and wings are black with hints of white; chest and stomach, dull yellow; stout pale yellow bill and dark pink feet.
Female: Silver grey with light hints of dull yellow on neck and sides, tail and wings are black with white edges.

Did you know? The Evening Grosbeak was mostly seen in western Canada until recent times when it moved east and north and can now be found in many parts of Nova Scotia.

Voice: Call is a ringing *cleer* or *clee-ip*. When there is a flock of birds calling they sound like sleighbells.
Food: Seeds, insects various fruits and flower buds.
Nest/eggs: Loosely woven cup of twigs and moss lined with small roots. Conifer tree or shrub, in colonies. 3-4 eggs.

Pine Grosbeak
Pinicola enucleator

Observation Calendar

J F M A M J J A S O N D

Male: Brilliant rose red and black that fades into grey just below chest; wings black with two white bars; tail black with hints of brown; grey chin with red highlights contrast with black stout bill; feet and legs black.

Female: Similar to male except soft grey all over except for hints of olive yellow at head and rump.

Voice: A three-note sweet musical song *twee wee tee*. Middle note is highest.

Food: A variety of insects, various fruits, seeds and flower buds.

Nest/eggs: Bulky nest of mosses, twigs, lichens and grass, lined with hair. Low in tree or shrub. 2-5 eggs.

Rose-breasted Grosbeak

Pheucticus ludovicianus

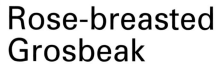

Observation Calendar
J F M A M J J A S O N D

Male: Large, pale yellow bill with black head; red V shape on chest; belly white with rust on either side; wings and tail black with white at edges of tail feathers visible in flight; white patches on wings; rump white; feet and legs charcoal.
Female: Buff eyebrow that extends to back of neck; brown head and back with shade of black; wings and tail brown with white edges; two white wing bars; chest and belly speckled brown; feet and legs charcoal.

Did you know? The Rose-breasted Grosbeak is a fierce competitor when mating, clashing violently with other males. However, when it comes time to sitting on the nest, the males have been known to sing.

Voice: Similar to a robin but rapid notes that are continuous *cheer-e-ly cheer-e-ly.* Call is *chink chink.*
Food: A variety of insects, tree buds, fruit and wild seeds.
Nest/eggs: Woven grass cup in fork of deciduous tree or shrub, close to the ground. 3-6 eggs.

Gray Partridge
Perdix perdix

Size Identification

Foot: Anisodactyl

Observation Calendar

J F M A M J J A S O N D

Male/Female: Overall grey with brick red face and throat, reddish brown banding on wings, feet and legs yellow; bill pale yellow. *In-flight:* Brick red tail feathers are exposed.

Egg: Actual Size

Did you know? These game birds were introduced to North America from Europe.

Voice: Call is a *keee ukk.*
Food: A variety of seeds, grain, leaves and insects.
Nest/eggs: Hollow in ground, in thick wooded areas, under felled log or rock, lined with leaves, pine needles and feathers. 9-12 eggs.

Nesting Location

Ruffed Grouse
Bonasa umbellus

Observation Calendar
J F M A M J J A S O N D

Male: Distinctive crest on head; overall brown speckled bird with black shoulder band on back of neck; tail is grey with broad black band at tip; eye brown; feet and legs grey.
Female: Similar to male except browner and more barring on underside; black shoulder band is narrower.

Did you know? The female will act injured if there is a threat near the nest.

Voice: An alarm note of *qit qit*. Cooing by female.
Food: A variety of insects, seeds, tree buds, leaves and berries.
Nest/eggs: Hollow under log or near the base of a tree lined with leaves, pine needles and feathers. 9-12 eggs.

Spruce Grouse
Falcipennis canadensis

Foot: Anisodactyl

Observation Calendar

J F M A M J J A S O N D

Male: Black chest and chin; overall black speckled with larger white areas on front; feet and legs charcoal; red head patch; small black curved bill; tail black with brown tips.
Female: Similar to male overall except black is replaced with brown or grey.

Egg: Actual Size

Did you know? A trademark for grouse is the drumming sound they can create by quick beating of their wings that is done in courtship or territorial display.

Confirmed breeding grounds have been found in Kejimkujik National Park and parts of Cape Breton.

Voice: Mostly silent birds with occasional hissing.
Food: Ground insects, buds of conifers, wild berries, a variety of seeds.
Nest/eggs: Hollow on ground lined with dead leaves, grass, pine needles and feathers, preferring locations under conifers and in tangled bushes. 4-10 eggs.

Nesting Location

Broad-winged Hawk

Buteo platypterus

Observation Calendar
J F M A M J J A S O N D

Male/Female: In flight: Brownish red banding on chest and belly; wings white with faint banding; tail broad with large black banding against white; chin white; top of head brown. Perched: Dark brown wings; yellow eye ringed in black; feet and legs yellow; bill charcoal grey.

Did you know? In September hawks sometimes gather together in flocks of hundreds.

Seen in deciduous forests in mainland Nova Scotia.

Voice: Whistle that is high-pitched *peee peeeeee.*
Food: Small mammals, birds, reptiles and amphibians.
Nest/eggs: Small stick, twigs, and leaves, lined with bark, in main supporting branches of tree, against trunk. 2-3 eggs.

Cooper's Hawk

Accipiter cooperii

Observation Calendar
J F M A M J J A S O N D

Male/Female: In flight: White chest and belly with rust banding down to lower belly; buff tail is long and rounded with faint charcoal banding; chin white; buff and white under wings with charcoal banding; grey on top of head. When in flight it has a steady wingbeat. Perched: Grey wings and tail with rust edging at ends; eyes are brick red; bill black and yellow; feet and legs yellow with rust feathers banded white down to knee.

Voice: Call is a loud *kek kek kek*.
Food: Small birds.
Nest/eggs: Large nest built of sticks and twigs, in conifer tree, 6-18 metres above ground. 4-5 eggs.

Northern Goshawk
Accipiter gentilis

Foot: Anisodactyl

Egg: 80%

Observation Calendar

J F M A M J J A S O N D

Male/Female: In flight: Underside is grey with dark brown banding overall; tail long with rich red along edges; buff eyebrow runs to back of neck. Perched: Dark brown wings with buff edging; eye brick red; bill black with yellow at base; feet and legs yellow with white feathers, banded brown reaching down to knees.

Did you know? This is an aggressive bird that has the ability fly in densely wooded areas chasing small birds.

Voice: Loud *keeek keeek keeek*.
Food: Small birds and occasional small mammals, such as squirrels.
Nest/eggs: Stick nest lodged in crotch of tree against the trunk, lined with bark, feathers and down. 3-4 eggs.

Nesting Location

Northern Harrier (Marsh Hawk)

Circus cyaneus

Foot: Anisodactyl

Egg: 90%

J F M A M J J A S O N D

Male: In flight: White underside with black and rust speckles; head is grey; black on tips of wings; orange feet; wings are V-shaped in flight. Perched: Grey head with white face mask; yellow eyes; thin rust banding down front; white rump.
Female: Slightly larger than male with brown overall; buff face disk around cheeks; buff under chin and belly is banded with brown; bill grey; yellow eyes.

Did you know? While gliding over meadows, the Northern Harrier's wings take a V-shape, making it easy to identify.

Voice: Relatively quiet bird with occasional screams of alarm.
Food: A variety of small mammals and birds.
Nest/eggs: On or near ground, built of sticks, straw and grasses. 4-5 eggs.

Nesting Location

Red-shouldered Hawk
Buteo lineatus

Observation Calendar

J F M A M J J A S O N D

Male/Female: In flight: Rust red chest lightly banded with buff, pale crescent on outer area of wings. Perched: Red brick shoulder patch; black wings with streaks of white; head buff with dark brown streaking; tail dark with white banding; bill black with yellow at base, feet and legs yellow with buff feathers banded with rust that reach just above feet; eyes dark.

Did you know? Red-shouldered Hawks return to the same nesting site year after year.

Voice: Decreasing scream *ke-er-ke-er-ke-er.*
Food: Amphibians, snakes, small mammals, small birds and insects.
Nest/eggs: Sticks and twigs lined with bark, feathers and down, built close to trunk in cavity of tree, near swamps and bogs. 3 eggs.

Red-tailed Hawk
Buteo jamaicensis

Observation Calendar
J F M A M J J A S O N D

Male/Female: In flight: Tail will appear faint red depending on light; broad wings and belly, white banded with charcoal. Perched: Wings are dark brown with buff edges; eyes brick red; bill yellow and black; feet and legs yellow with white feathers banded brown/charcoal reach to knees; tail brick red.

Voice: A scream that is downward *keeer er er.*
Food: Small mammals, amphibians, nestlings, insects, reptiles and birds.
Nest/eggs: Flat and shallow, stick and twig nest, lined with moss and evergreen sprigs, on rocky ledges or in trees that are in the open, 10-30 metres above ground. 2 eggs.

Rough-legged Hawk
Buteo lagopus

Similar to Red-tailed hawk; charcoal grey wings and back; chest white with black bands, belly black; white tail with one dark band at tip; beak black.

Sharp-shinned Hawk

Accipiter striatus

Size Identification

Foot: Anisodactyl

Egg: Actual Size

Backyard Feeder

Observation Calendar

J F M A M J J A S O N D

Male/Female: In flight: Small hawk with rust chest banded with buff; long square tail is white with charcoal banding; wings dark brown and rounded; top of head dark brown. Perched: Brick-red eyes with brown band just below eye; bill is black with yellow base; feet and legs yellow; white feathers extend out of rust coloured belly.

Did you know? Over the past few years there has been a dramatic decrease in the eastern population. This may be directly related to the decrease in songbirds that it hunts.

Voice: A quick high pitched *kik kik kik*.
Food: Small songbirds.
Nest/eggs: Broad platforms of twigs and sticks in conifers or deciduous trees built against the trunk, lined with bark. 4-5 eggs.

Nesting Location

Ruby-throated Hummingbird

Archilochus colubris

Observation Calendar

J F M A M J J A S O N D

Male: Dark green head which is iridescent in parts; red throat begins darker under chin; white collar, breast and belly; wings and notched tail black; iridescent green on back; black bill is long and thin; small white area behind eyes; feet and legs black.

Female: Head, back and parts of tail are bright iridescent green; white throat, chest and belly; wings and tail black with white outer tips; black bill is long and thin; small white area behind eyes; feet and legs black.

Voice: A low *hummmmmm* followed occasionally by a angry sounding squeak or chattering.

Food: Nectar from a variety of plants including thistles, jewelweed, trumpet vines and other blossoms, occasionally insects.

Nest/eggs: Small, tightly woven cup with deep cavity built with fibres and attached with spider web, lined with plant down, covered on the outside with lichens, in tree or shrub, 3-6 metres above ground. 2 eggs.

Blue Jay
Cyanocitta cristata

Observation Calendar
J F M A M J J A S O N D

Male/Female: Bright blue crested head with black band running through eye to just under crest on back of neck; black band continues along side of neck on both sides to chest; white under chin; back is blue; wings and tail are blue banded with black and tipped with white at ends; black bill is large with light feathers covering nostril area; feet and legs black.

Did you know? The Blue Jay has a bad reputation for eating eggs of other birds, and even their young.

Voice: Call is *jay jay jay*, plus many other calls including mimicking hawks.

Food: Omnivorous — in summer months the Blue Jay feasts on just about anything, including spiders, snails, salamanders, frogs, seeds and caterpillars. In winter months they supplement their diet with acorns and other nuts stored in tree cavities earlier in the year.

Nest/eggs: Bulky nest of sticks, leaves, string and moss lined with small roots, well hidden, 1-15 metres above ground, in tree or shrub. 3-4 eggs.

Gray Jay
Perisoreus canadensis

Size Identification

Foot: Anisodactyl

Egg: Actual Size

Backyard Feeder

Birdhouse Nester

Nesting Location

Observation Calendar

J F M A M J J A S O N D

Male/Female: White forehead with a dark grey patch on head which varies depending on geographic location; grey back, wings and tail with white underparts; feet and legs are dark grey, black bill is short and sharp; white cheeks, wings and tail are edged with white and grey.

Did you know? Its scientific name means "heap up." The Gray Jay likes to cache heaps of food at every chance it gets.

Voice: A variety of calls similar to a hawk but most recognizable call is very loud *churrrr* plus a series of whistles and cooing.

Food: Omnivorous — a variety of items including insects, berries, fruit, small mammals, reptiles, amphibians, and human food waste.

Nest/eggs: Bulky cup built with sticks, spider's web, hair and fur, lined with bark, in conifer tree or shrub near trunk, up to 10 metres above ground. 3-4 eggs.

Dark-eyed Junco

Junco hyemalis

Observation Calendar

J F M A M J J A S O N D

Male: Dark charcoal overall with white belly; short sharp bill is pale yellow with black at end; feet and legs dark grey; tail has white outer feathers that can be seen in flight.
Female: May be slightly paler than male.

Did you know? Although there are many different sub-species, the slate-coloured species is the only one found in Nova Scotia.

Voice: Song is a trill in short phrases. Calls are *tsip, zeeet* or *keew keew*.
Food: A variety of insects, weed seeds and wild fruit.
Nest/eggs: Large and compact built with grass, rootlets and hair, lined with hair, concealed low to or on ground. 4-5 eggs.

American Kestrel

Falco sparverius

Foot: Anisodactyl

Egg: Actual Size

Observation Calendar
J F M A M J J A S O N D

Male/Female: In flight: overall buff with black speckles; distinctive black banding on face. Perched: charcoal wings with black, separated banding; back rust with black banding; grey top of head with rust patch on top; black bands running down cheeks against white; bill black/charcoal with yellow at base; feet and legs orange; tail deep rust with broad black tip.

Voice: Rapid *klee klee klee* or *kily kily kily.*
Food: Mice, voles, insects and small birds.
Nest/eggs: In cavity of tree or man-made boxes, little or no nesting material. 3-5 eggs

Birdhouse Nester

Nesting Location

Eastern Kingbird
Tyrannus tyrannus

Observation Calendar

J F M A M J J A S O N D

Male/Female: Black head, back, wings and tail; white chin, chest and belly; wings have white along edge and tail has white band along tip; feet and legs black.

Did you know? Size does not matter to the Eastern Kingbird: they will attack crows, ravens, hawks and owls to defend their territory. Seen in the Wolfville area, and near Amherst.

Voice: Several different calls including *tzi tzee* as a true song. Also a *kitter kitter kitter* when threatened.
Food: Flying insects and fruit in late summer.
Nest/eggs: Bulky cup built with weed stalks, grass and moss, in branches of tree or shrub, 3-6 metres above ground. 3-5 eggs.

Belted Kingfisher
Ceryle alcyon

Foot: Anisodactyl

Observation Calendar
J F M A M J J A S O N D

Egg: Actual Size

Male: A large head and long black bill, crested blue/black head, very short blue tail; wings black with white bands; chest white; white collar wraps around neck with blue band that wraps around chest; feet and legs charcoal.
Female: Same as male except a rust colour breast band.

Did you know? Belted Kingfishers teach their young to dive for food by catching a fish, stunning it, then placing it on the surface of the water. The young birds then practise diving for it.

Voice: A continuous deep rattle during flight.
Food: Small fish, amphibians, reptiles, insects and crayfish.
Nest/eggs: A cavity or tunnel excavated in a bank near a river or lake. 5-8 eggs.

Nesting Location

Golden-crowned Kinglet

Regulus satrapa

Observation Calendar

J F M A M J J A S O N D

Male: One of the smallest woodland birds with black head stripes that set off its crown patch of orange with yellow edges; neck and back olive-grey; wings and tail black with olive along edges; feet and legs black; pale grey wingbars; pale eyebrow.

Female: Similar to male except patch on top is yellow.

Did you know? Their movements on a tree make them easy to spot. They flutter their wings as they look for insects.

Voice: Very high pitched dropping to a quick chatter. The song is so highly pitched that some people cannot hear its song.

Food: A variety of insects, spiders, fruits and seeds.

Nest/eggs: Deep cup built with moss and lichen at top, lined with black rootlets and feathers suspended from conifer branch, up to 30 metres above ground. 5-11 eggs.

Ruby-crowned Kinglet

Regulus calendula

Size Identification

Foot: Anisodactyl

Observation Calendar

J F M A M J J A S O N D

Male: Olive-grey overall with white eye ring broken at top; crested with red patch on head; chin and neck are lighter olive-grey, feet and legs black; wings and tail black with white edges; white bands on wings.
Female: Similar to male except for no red patch on top of head.

Egg: Actual Size

Did you know? The ruby red top on the male is hard to see except when he is courting when it will flare up.

Voice: High pitched *tee tee tee* followed by a lower *tew tew tew* and ending with a chatter.
Food: Insects, insect eggs, spiders, fruits and seeds.
Nest/eggs: Deep woven cup built with moss, lichen at top and lined with small black roots and feathers, suspended from conifer branch. 5-10 eggs.

Nesting Location

Horned Lark

Eremophila alpestris

Observation Calendar

J F M A M J J A S O N D

Male/Female: Dull brown on top; chest and belly white; wings and tail brown and black; distinctive black facial marks which include small horns (feathers) on either side of its head; chin pale yellow with black band above running through eye and down; feet and legs black.

Did you know? The horns are not always visible but a quick way to identify the Horned Lark is that on the ground it walks and does not hop, like most small birds.

Breeding grounds near Greenwood Air Base and Halifax and Sydney airports.

Voice: Soft twittering *tsee titi* or *zzeeet*.
Food: A variety of insects, seeds and grains.
Nest/eggs: Hollow in ground under grass tuft, made of stems and leaves, lined with grass. 3-5 eggs.

Lapland Longspur

Calcarius lapponicus

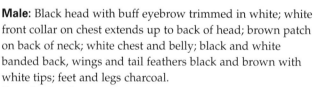

Observation Calendar

J F M A M J J A S O N D

Male: Black head with buff eyebrow trimmed in white; white front collar on chest extends up to back of head; brown patch on back of neck; white chest and belly; black and white banded back, wings and tail feathers black and brown with white tips; feet and legs charcoal.
Female: Similar to male except solid blacks are broken up by white speckles; belly grey and body is overall brown.

Voice: Song is whistle *ticki ticki teew*, sung while in flight.
Food: A variety of insects, spiders and seeds.
Nest/eggs: Cup nest low to ground in tree or shrub. 3-5 eggs.

Eastern Meadowlark
Sturnella magna

Observation Calendar
J F M A M J J A S O N D

Male/Female: Bright yellow chin and throat separated by a V-shaped black collar; black on top of head with white cheeks; yellow and black band runs through eye; sides white with black speckles; back and wings black and brown with white edges; feet and legs grey; black bill is long and thin with gray underside.

Voice: Song is *teee yuuu teee yaar* repeated two to eight times.
Food: A variety of insects including grubs, beetles, grasshoppers and caterpillars. Also eats seeds and grain.
Nest/eggs: Bulky cup in hollow on the ground in pastures, fields and marshes. Dome-shaped with a roof of interwoven grasses. 3-5 eggs.

Purple Martin
Progne subis

Foot: Anisodactyl

Observation Calendar
J F M A M J J A S O N D

Male: Very shiny, dark purple overall, with black wings and tail; black bill is short and slightly curved; feet and legs reddish black; wings very long reaching to tip of tail when folded.
Female: Dull purple head and back with black wings and tail; chest and chin grey; belly white with black speckles; feet and legs black.

Breeds only in northern areas.

Voice: Call is high pitched *cheer cheer.*
Food: Flying insects.
Nest/eggs: Deep cup in cavity lined with grass and leaves, usually in large colonies. Nests in gourds and special martin houses. 3-8 eggs.

Egg: Actual Size

Birdhouse Nester

Nesting Location

Common Nighthawk
Chordeiles minor

Observation Calendar

J F M A M J J A S O N D

Male: Grey and black speckled bird with long thin wings; white collar wraps around to bottom of neck; legs and feet light grey. When in flight white bands near tail are visible.

Did you know? This bird eats in flight by scooping insects into their large mouths. You can often see nighthawks feeding near lights on warm nights.

Seen in inland areas, especially in Kejimkujik National Park and in Cape Breton.

Voice: A nasal sounding *peeent*.
Food: Flying insects.
Nest/eggs: In depression on the ground, often in gravel, with lining. 2 eggs.

Red-breasted Nuthatch

Sitta canadensis

Foot: Anisodactyl

Observation Calendar
J F M A M J J A S O N D

Male: Small round bird with black stripe over top of head and white stripe underneath running over eye to back of head, followed by another black band running through eye; white cheeks turn to rust at neck and continue rust to chest and belly; back is grey-blue; wings and tail grey becoming black at ends; black bill is often white on underside; feet and legs brown-black.

Female: Similar to male except for grey cap and light underside.

Egg: Actual Size

Did you know? The Red-breasted Nuthatch will smear pitch at the entrance to its nest, although it is not known why.

Voice: A tin-whistle call and an occasional loud *knack knack*.
Food: Seeds, insects and flying insects
Nest/eggs: Cup lined with grass, moss and feathers, in excavated cavity or crevice of tree. 1-12 metres above ground. 4-7 eggs.

Backyard Feeder

Birdhouse Nester

Nesting Location

White-breasted Nuthatch

Sitta carolinensis

Observation Calendar
J F M A M J J A S O N D

Male: Shiny black on top of head running down the back, turning to lighter blue-grey on back; white face and neck which runs down chest and belly; slight rust colours on sides, wings and tail are blue-grey with white edges; feet and legs black.
Female: Similar to male except top of head and back are lighter grey.

Did you know? These little birds are known for their ability to run down tree trunks headfirst, at a very fast pace.

Voice: Nesting pairs keep in contact with one another with a deep sounding *aank aank* but also chatter a soft *ip ip.*
Food: Spiders, insects, seeds, insect eggs and acorns.
Nest/eggs: Cup lined with twig, feathers, small roots, fur and hair, in natural cavity or crevice of tree, 4-15 metres above ground. 5-10 eggs.

Osprey
Pandion haliaetus

Foot: Zygodactyl

Egg: 70%

Observation Calendar

J F M A M J J A S O N D

Male/Female: In flight: White belly and chest; wings grey with black banding; white wing underparts connect to chest; black band running through eye; large black bill; tail grey with black banding. Perched: Black back and wings with thin white line running above wing; eye yellow with black band running through and down to cheek; chin white; top of head white with black patches.
Female: More streaked then males.

Seen along the Atlantic coastline, including Halifax Harbour.

Voice: A loud chirp which trails off or ascending *squeeeee* during courtship displays.
Food: Various small fish.
Nest/eggs: Constructed of twigs and sticks, lined with sod, grass and vines in upper parts of trees and on top of poles, 60 feet above ground 2-3 eggs.

Nesting Location

Barred Owl

Strix varia

Foot: Zygodactyl

Egg: 60%

Observation Calendar
J F M A M J J A S O N D

Male/Female: Large dark eyes set in buff and rich brown; white bands extend out from face, down the back including wings and tail feathers; chest white with rich brown feathers in columns; bill is small yellow hook shape.

Did you know? The Barred Owls' ears are positioned differently on either side of the head. This allows for better hearing in total darkness.

Voice: Very rhythmic hoots in series of four or five at a time.
Food: Small mammals
Nest/eggs: Cavity of tree or abandoned hawksÌ or crowsÌ nests; no lining added. 2-3 eggs.

Birdhouse Nester

Nesting Location

Great Horned Owl
Bubo virginianus

Egg: 70%

Observation Calendar

J F M A M J J A S O N D

Male/Female: Very recognizable ear tufts that sit wide apart; bright yellow eyes surrounded by rust colour; grey and brown overall with black bands.

Voice: Hoot consists of several *hoo hoo hoo hoo hoo hoo*. Male is deeper then female.

Food: Small mammals, birds and reptiles.

Nest/eggs: Nests in a deserted hawk's, heron's or crow's nest with very little material added. Occasionally will lay eggs on ground amongst bones, skulls and bits of fur. 1-3 eggs.

Nesting Location

Northern Saw-whet Owl

Aegolius acadicus

Observation Calendar
J F M A M J J A S O N D

Male/Female: Yellow eyes that are surrounded by a reddish brown facial disk; chest white with brown streaks running length of body; feet and legs grey.

Small populations scattered throughout the province.

Voice: Whistled song repeated *too too too*.
Food: Diet consists mainly of small mammals, including voles, chipmunks, and bats.
Nest/eggs: Cavity of dead tree, 4-18 metres above ground. No material added. 2-6 eggs.

Boreal Owl

Aegolius funereus

Slightly larger than Saw-whet owl, similar markings, with dark border on facial disks, spotted forehead, yellow bill. Seen only in northern regions of Cape Breton.

Short-eared Owl

Asio flammeus

Foot: Zygodactyl

Egg: Actual Size

Observation Calendar

J F M A M J J A S O N D

Male/Female: Dark brown overall with buff banding on back; small ear tufts black and buff directly above eyes on top of head (rarely seen); wings and tail feathers dark brown with buff bands; light buff chest and belly with brown streaks; long wings tipped black at the ends; eyes brilliant yellow surrounded by black; bill black; feet and legs black.

Did you know? The Short-eared Owl flies low to the ground when hunting but is able to hover momentarily when prey is spotted.

Small populations seen in Wolfville, Glace Bay, Pugwash and Amherst areas.

Voice: Raspy *yip yip yip.*
Food: Small mammals, mostly voles, songbirds and game birds.
Nest/eggs: Slight depression hidden in grass. Lined with grass and feathers. 4-9 eggs.

Nesting Location

Eastern Wood-Pewee

Contopus virens

Observation Calendar

J F M A M J J A S O N D

Male/Female: Olive-grey overall with head that is crested at back; wings black and dark grey with two white bars; throat and chest white; belly slightly yellow or white; tail charcoal; bill black on top and yellow underside; feet and legs black.

Did you know? The Wood-Pewee changes its voice in morning and evening, converting its song into a slow verse.

Voice: A soft whistle *pee-a-wee pee-awee* repeated without any pause early in the morning.
Food: Flies, beetles, bees, ants and other insects.
Nest/eggs: Shallow cup built with grass, spider's web and fibres lined with hair, covered outside with lichens, on horizontal branch of tree far out from trunk, 5-20 metres above ground. 3-5 eggs.

Common Pheasant
Phasianus colchicus

Observation Calendar
J F M A M J J A S O N D

Male: Green iridescent head with distinctive red wattles (patches around eye), white collar, overall body is mixture of grey, black and brown; long tail feathers brown with black banding; feet and legs charcoal grey; pale yellow bill.
Female: Grey-brown overall with dark markers over entire body; pale yellow bill; small red wattle above eye.

Did you know? This chicken-like bird gets into some real cock fights in early spring, jumping, pecking, clawing for their right to territory.

Voice: Similar to a wild turkey gobble at a higher pitch.
Food: Seeds, insects, grains and berries.
Nest/eggs: Shallow bowl on ground lined with weed, grass and leaves. 6-15 eggs.

Eastern Phoebe

Sayornis phoebe

Size Identification

Foot: Anisodactyl

Egg: Actual Size

Observation Calendar
J F M A M J J A S O N D

Male/Female: Grey-brown head and back with white throat, chest and belly; feet and legs black; white wing bands; pale yellow belly.

Did you know? One quick way to identify this bird is to watch the greyish brown tail bobbing up and down.

Seen in parts of mainland Nova Scotia, including the Annapolis Valley and the South Shore.

Voice: Song is rough sounding *fee bee fee bee*. Call is *wit*.
Food: Flying insects as well as ground insects.
Nest/eggs: Large shelf structure built with weeds, grass, fibres and mud, covered with moss, lined with grass and hair. 3-6 eggs.

Nesting Location

Common Raven

Corvus corax

Egg: 80%

Observation Calendar

J F M A M J J A S O N D

Male/Female: Shiny, black bird overall with a blue tint; feet and legs black; black bill is long and wide and has been described as a "Roman nose"; rounded tail.

Voice: Variety of calls including buzzing, croaks and gulps.
Food: A variety of insects, carrion, small mammals and food waste.
Nest/eggs: Large basket of twigs, sticks, vines, hair and moss, lined with animal hair, on ledge, in tree or shrub. 3-4 eggs.

Nesting Location

Northern Shrike

Lanius excubitor

Size Identification

Foot: Anisodactyl

Egg: Actual Size

Observation Calendar
J F M A M J J A S O N D

Male/Female: Black mask that may be dull at times; long sharp hooked black bill; head and back grey; throat, chest and belly soft grey with light grey banding from chest to lower belly; feet and legs black; wings and tail black with white edges.

Did you know? This bird is more like a hawk or owl because of its diet and hunting technique. Once the Northern Shrike has caught its prey it will often hang it in a thorny bush, saving it for later.

Voice: A light song *queeedle queeedle* along with *tsurp-see tsurpsee.*
Food: Small birds and mammals but diet consists mainly of grasshoppers, locust, crickets and other large insects.
Nest/eggs: Bulky woven cup built with sticks, twigs, grass and small roots, lined with cotton, feather and bark, in tree or shrub, up to 10 metres above ground. 4-7 eggs. (Does not breed in Nova Scotia.)

Nesting Location

Pine Siskin

Carduelis pinus

Size Identification

Foot: Anisodactyl

Observation Calendar

J F M A M J J A S O N D

Male/Female: Brown with buff chest and belly banded with brown; long pointed bill is grey, wings and tail dark with yellow edges; feet and legs grey.

Egg: Actual Size

Did you know? Two points of identification of the Pine Siskin are its size and the song, which it sings in flight.

Voice: Light rasping *tit i tit* and louder *cleeeip*. Similar to a Goldfinch but deeper and coarser.

Food: Conifer seeds, weed seeds, nectar, flower buds and a variety of insects.

Nest/eggs: Large shallow cup built with twigs, grass, moss, lichen, bark and small roots, lined with moss, hair and feathers in a conifer tree well out from trunk, 6 metres above ground. 2-6 eggs.

Backyard Feeder

Nesting Location

American Tree Sparrow

Spizella arborea

Foot: Anisodactyl

Egg: Actual Size

Backyard Feeder

Observation Calendar
J F M A M J J A S O N D

Male/Female: Rust on top of head with light grey face, rust band running through eye; chin, chest and belly grey with a faint dark grey spot on chest; wings and tail brown and black with white edge; two white wing bars; short pointed bill is grey on top with yellow underside; feet and legs are red-black, rump grey.

Seen in Cape Breton Highlands National Park.

Voice: Call is *te el wit.*
Food: A variety of weed seeds and tree seeds.
Nest/eggs: Cup nest, low in tree and shrub. 4 eggs. (Does not breed in Nova Scotia.)

Nesting Location

Chipping Sparrow
Spizella passerina

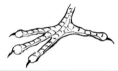

Observation Calendar
J F M A M J J A S O N D

Male/Female: *Summer:* Bright rust crown with grey face that has a black band running through eye; short pointed bill is black; chin white changing to grey for chest and belly; feet and legs pink with black; white eyebrow; wings and tail black with brown and white edges; back brown banding with black. *Winter:* Rust crown becomes duller turning brown with black streaks; bill is pale yellow and black; eyebrow changes to buff; underside changes to buff.

Voice: Song is short trill.
Food: A variety of insects on the ground and occasionally snatches flying insects.
Nest/eggs: Cup built with grass, weed stalks and small roots, lined with hair and grass, low in tree or shrub, up to 8 metres above ground. 4 eggs.

House Sparrow
Passer domesticus

Size Identification

Foot: Anisodactyl

Egg: Actual Size

Observation Calendar
J F M A M J J A S O N D

Male: Rich brown on head with white cheeks; wings and tail striped with black; two distinct white wing bands; rump grey; throat and chest black which turns grey at belly; bill black; feet and legs pink.

Female: Dull brown with buff chin, chest and belly; light buff coloured eyebrows and yellow/grey bill.

Did you know? In the mid-1800s eight pairs of House Sparrows were brought to North America from Europe to help control cankerworms in crops. The first attempt failed but this sparrow has now become one of the most common birds in cities and towns.

Voice: Repeated *chureep, chirup.*
Food: Insects, seed, grain and food waste.
Nest/eggs: Takes over nests from other birds. Usually a large untidy ball of grass, weeds, some hair, feathers. 3-7 eggs.

Backyard Feeder

Birdhouse Nester

Nesting Location

Lincoln's Sparrow

Melospiza lincolnii

Observation Calendar

J F M A M J J A S O N D

Male/Female: Rust on top of head with thin grey central streak; dark grey face; buff across chest and down sides of belly with fine black streaking; belly white; feet and legs pink; wing and tail feathers black with brown edges.

Seen in central and northern areas of the province.

Voice: Wild mixture of trills and buzzing. Calls include *tsup and zeee.*
Food: A variety of weed seeds and insects.
Nest/eggs: Flat ground in bundle of grass. Built with grass, moss and lichen, lined with fine grass. 3-6 eggs.

Savannah Sparrow
Passerculus sandwichensis

Observation Calendar
J F M A M J J A S O N D

Male/Female: Black, brown and white central stripe on head; back brown with black banding; chin, chest and belly streaked with black and brown; wings and tail black with brown edges; tail is notched; bright yellow eyebrow; feet and legs red; short pointed bill is black and pink; white eye ring.

Voice: A faint, lisping *tsit tsit tsit tseeeee tsaaaay.*
Food: Main diet consist of weed seeds but will eat a variety of insects, spiders and snails.
Nest/eggs: Scratched hollow in ground filled with grass, lined with finer grass, hair and small roots. 3-6 eggs

Song Sparrow
Melospiza melodia

Size Identification

Foot: Anisodactyl

Egg: Actual Size

Backyard Feeder

Nesting Location

Observation Calendar

J F M A M J J A S O N D

Male/Female: Brown head and back streaked with black; buff-grey eyebrow extending to back of neck; brown band running through eye; chin, chest and belly are white with brown-black banding running down to lower belly; short pointed bill is black on top with yellow underside; red-brown crown with central white stripe; wings and tail brown with white edges; feet and legs pink; long rounded tail.

Did you know? Thoreau 'interpreted' this sparrow's song as "Maids! Maids! Maids! hang up your teakettle-ettle-ettle."

Voice: Call is a variety which includes *tsip* and *tchump*. Song is a variety of rich notes.
Food: A variety of insects, weed seeds and fruit.
Nest/eggs: Cup close to ground with weeds, leaves and bark, lined with grass roots and hair, in tree or shrub, less than 4 metres from ground. 3-5 eggs.

Swamp Sparrow
Melospiza georgiana

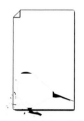

Size Identification

Foot: Anisodactyl

Egg: Actual Size

Observation Calendar
J F M A M J J A S O N D

Male/Female: *Summer:* Top of head is reddish brown and black; face grey with black streaks; black bill is small and sharp; chin and chest white-grey with rust along sides; back brown with black banding; wings and tail feathers brown with black ends and white edges; feet and legs pink; grey eyebrows. *Winter:* Similar to summer but both sides of chest turn darker brown and top of head is streaked with black and brown with grey central stripe.

Put on your hip waders to spot this bird. They spend their summers near swamps and bogs.

Voice: Song is an unbroken musical trill. Call is *chip.*
Food: A variety of insects and seeds.
Nest/eggs: Bulky cup built with grass, lined with finer grass, in tussock of grass or in low shrub. 3-6 eggs.

Nesting Location

Vesper Sparrow

Pooecetes gramineus

Size Identification

Foot: Anisodactyl

Egg: Actual Size

Observation Calendar
J F M A M J J A S O N D

Male/Female: Light grey overall with very fine streaks of black running down entire body; short pointed bill black on top with grey underside; feet and legs grey; back banded with black; wings and tail dark grey with white edges; white ring, and small chestnut patch near shoulder; white tail feathers are revealed in flight.

Did you know? The Vesper Sparrow earned its name from its song that may be heard in the evening — at vespers, when evening prayers were said in the monasteries.

Seen in the Amherst area and a few other places around the province.

Voice: A whistle of two beats, with the second being higher, followed by trills.
Food: A variety of insects, weed seeds and grain.
Nest/eggs: Depression in ground with grass, stalks, and small roots, and lined with the same. 4 eggs.

Nesting Location

White-throated Sparrow

Zonotrichia albicollis

Observation Calendar

J F M A M J J A S O N D

Male/Female: Top of head is black with white central stripe; white eyebrows on either side that begin with yellow tint; black band running through eye followed by grey cheeks; small white bib under chin; grey chest; white belly with faint banding; wings and tail feathers black and brown with white edges; feet pink; back brown banded with black.

Voice: Whistle is *teeet teeet tetodi tetodi teetodi.* Calls are *tseet.*
Food: A variety of insects, grain, weed seeds and fruit.
Nest/eggs: Cup built of grass, small roots, pine needles, twigs, bark and moss, lined with small roots, hair and grass. 3-5 eggs.

Bank Swallow

Riparia riparia

Foot: Anisodactyl

Observation Calendar

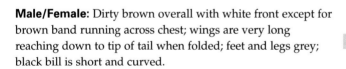

J F M A M J J A S O N D

Male/Female: Dirty brown overall with white front except for brown band running across chest; wings are very long reaching down to tip of tail when folded; feet and legs grey; black bill is short and curved.

Egg: Actual Size

Voice: A variety of calls including *tchirrt tchirrt* and long twittering.

Food: Flying insects as well as a variety of other insects. Main diet consists of dragonflies, flies, mayflies and beetles.

Nest/eggs: Earth tunnel lined with grass and straw along bank of water. 4-6 eggs.

Nesting Location

Barn Swallow
Hirundo rustica

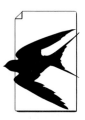

Observation Calendar
J F M A M J J A S O N D

Male: Dark blue iridescent from top of head, shoulders, down back and top of wings; chin and chest rust colour that fades to white at belly; wings are very long and extend to tips of tail which is forked with long feathers at either end that can be seen when bird is in flight; feet and legs charcoal; black and cream bill. When bird is in flight a band of white can be seen at end of wings.
Female: Same markings but duller.

Did you know? Barn Swallows are amazing to watch as they skim over water and pick insects off the surface. In the evening they hunt mosquitoes.

Voice: A soft twittering *kvik kvik wit wit.*
Food: A variety of insects.
Nest/eggs: Mud and straw lined with feathers, in buildings, under bridges, in cliffs and caves. 4-5 eggs.

Cliff Swallow
Petrochelidon pyrrhonota

Size Identification

Foot: Anisodactyl

Observation Calendar
J F M A M J J A S O N D

Egg: Actual Size

Male/Female: Overall black with buff rump and brick red cheeks; white patch on forehead; belly white; back has variable amounts of white streaks; feet and legs grey; tail black, square at end.

Did you know? Nest sights can be a little competitive and the birds will steal nesting grasses and twigs from each other's nests.

Voice: A long *chuuurrrr* and a deeper *nyeeew*.
Food: A variety of insects.
Nest/eggs: Mud lined with grass, hair and feathers, under bridges, in cliffs and buildings. 3-6 eggs.

Nesting Location

Tree Swallow
Tachycineta bicolor

Observation Calendar
J F M A M J J A S O N D

Male/Female: Dark iridescent blue on head, neck, back, wings and tail; bright white chin, chest and belly; black bill is short and slightly curved; wings are very long reaching down to tip of tail when folded; feet and legs charcoal.

Did you know? The Tree Swallow is the only swallow that eats berries in the place of insects. This allows it to winter further north than its relatives.

Voice: Early morning song *wheet trit weet*, with an alarm call of *cheedeeep*.
Food: Flying insects and berries.
Nest/eggs: Cup in cavity of tree lined with grass and feathers, usually a woodpecker's old hole. 4-6 eggs.

Chimney Swift
Chaetura pelagica

Observation Calendar

J F M A M J J A S O N D

Male/Female: Dark charcoal on head, back, wings and tail; lighter on chest and throat; black bill is small with light grey on underside; feet and legs grey.

Did you know? A Chimney Swift is capable of snapping off tree twigs with its feet while in flight. It then takes the twig in its mouth and returns to its nest.

Voice: A very quick and repeated *chitter, chitter, chitter* with occasional *chip.*
Food: Flying insects such as moths and beetles.
Nest/eggs: Flimsy half cup attached by saliva to crevice or rock ledge in chimneys, barns, old buildings, and on rock formations. 3-6 eggs.

Scarlet Tanager
Piranga olivacea

Size Identification

Foot: Anisodactyl

Observation Calendar

J F M A M J J A S O N D

Male: Scarlet red from head to rump with dark black wings and tail; bill is dull yellow; feet and legs black.
Female: Olive-yellow overall with black-gray wings and tail.

In southern regions of the province, especially in urban areas.

Voice: Call is a Chip burr while its song is a buzzing *querit, queer, queery, querit, queer* that is well spaced out.
Food: A variety of insects and fruit.
Nest/eggs: Flat and flimsy cup nest on farthest branches in tree or shrub, sometimes far from the ground. 3-5 eggs

Egg: Actual Size

Nesting Location

American Robin
Turdus migratorius

Observation Calendar

| J | F | M | A | M | J | J | A | S | O | N | D |

Male: Charcoal/brown head with distinctive white above and below eye; back and wings charcoal brown with white edges; tail dark grey; neck dark grey with thin white banding; chest and belly brick red; feet and legs black; bill yellow with black at either end.
Female: Breast is slightly paler than male's.

Voice: Song is *cheerily cheerily cheerily* in a whistle tone.
Food: Earthworms, insects and fruit.
Nest/eggs: Deep cup built with weed stalks, cloth, string and mud, lined with grass, in evergreens and deciduous trees or shrubs. 4 eggs.

Gray Catbird
Dumetella carolinensis

Foot: Anisodactyl

Egg: Actual Size

Observation Calendar
J F M A M J J A S O N D

Male/Female: Distinctive black cap with overall grey body; brick red rump which is hidden most of the time; feet and legs grey with hints of pink.

Did you know? Catbirds actually migrate during the night hours and research indicates they use the moon for navigating.

Voice: A distinctive cat-like song: *meeow* and *kwut*.
Food: A variety of insects, spiders and wild berries.
Nest/eggs: Bulky deep cup built with twigs, vines, grass, paper and weeds lined with small roots, in dense thickets of tree or shrub, 1-3 metres above ground. 3-6 eggs.

Nesting Location

Hermit Thrush
Catharus guttatus

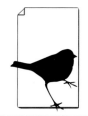

Foot: Anisodactyl

Egg: Actual Size

Observation Calendar

J F M A M J J A S O N D

Male/Female: Dusty brown head, neck and back that blends into a rust tail; white eye ring; wings rust when open with black ends; neck and chest white and dark spotted; underparts grey, feet and legs grey with pink; bill black and rust.

Did you know? Not surprisingly, a Hermit Thrush prefers the seclusion of deep wooded areas.

Voice: Sweet song with a variety of phrases. When disturbed it sounds a *kuk kuk kuk kuk*.
Food: A variety of insects, worms, caterpillars, snails and various fruits.
Nest/eggs: Bulky ground nest built with twig, bark, grass and moss and lined with conifer needles, fibre and small roots in damp and cool wooded areas. 3-4 eggs.

Nesting Location

Wood Thrush
Hylocichla mustelina

Observation Calendar
J F M A M J J A S O N D

Male/Female: Rust coloured head fades to a brown back; wings and tail dark brown with black ends; feet and legs grey with pink; black bill has light yellow on underside; white eye ring; chin and chest white with black spotting, underparts grey.

Voice: Suggestive of flute, the song is a series of varied phrases *ee oh lee ee oh lay.*
Food: A variety of insects on the ground and in trees.
Nest/eggs: Firm and compact cup built with grass, paper, moss, bark and mud, lined with small roots in tree or shrub, 2-15 metres above ground. 3-4 eggs

Swainson's Thrush
Hylocichla ustulata

More common than the Wood Thrush. Dull olive-brown on head and back; white eye ring; dark underparts and slightly smaller.

Red-eyed Vireo
Vireo olivaceus

Observation Calendar

J F M A M J J A S O N D

Male/Female: *Spring:* red eye encircled with thin line of black set against a wide white eyebrow that runs from bill to back of head; black bill; throat and chest white; feet and legs black; back and rump are olive green; wings and tail black with edges of olive green; eye is darker brown in winter.

Voice: The Red-eyed Vireo may sound over 40 different phrases in just 60 seconds, then begin all over again. A variety of short phrases which includes *cherrrwit chereeee cissy a witt teeeooo*.

Food: Small insects, berries and fruit.

Nest/eggs: Deep cup built with grass, paper, bark, rootlets, vine and decorated outside with spider's web and lichen, suspended in branches, .5-18 metres above ground. 2 eggs.

Solitary Vireo
Vireo solitarius

Observation Calendar
J F M A M J J A S O N D

Male/Female: Blue-grey head and back with shades of olive along back; eye is brown with distinctive white eyebrow encircling it; bill long and black; feet and legs charcoal; throat and belly white with olive along edges of belly; tail charcoal with white edges.

Did you know? Although these birds are not common in parks, they are very tame when approached. Sometimes they will continue to sit on their nest even in the presence of humans, while other birds would probably attack or retreat from the area with a few choice tweeeeps.

Voice: The song is a series of short whistled phrases interrupted by pauses, similar to the Red-Eyed Vireo but higher pitched and sweeter.
Food: Small insects and fruit.
Nest/eggs: Suspended basketlike cup built with bark, fibre, grass, small roots and hair in a tree, 1-6 metres above ground. 3-5 eggs.

Warbling Vireo

Vireo gilvus

Observation Calendar

J F M A M J J A S O N D

Egg: Actual Size

Male/Female: Grey and green head, neck and back; white eyebrow extending from black bill; white chin, breast and belly with variable amounts of yellow; feet and legs black; tail and wings black with white edging.

Seen only around Wolfville, Antigonish and parts of Cape Breton.

Voice: The best way to find a Warbling Vireo is to listen. This bird sings throughout the day with a beautiful warbling sound. Song is group of slurred phrases such as *brig-a-dier brig-a-dier brigate.*

Food: Small insects including caterpillars, beetles and moths, and some berries.

Nest/eggs: Tightly woven pensile cup built with bark, leaves, grass, feathers, plant down and spider's web, lined with stems and horsehair, suspended in tall trees at the edge of wooded area, well away from trunk. 3-5 eggs.

Nesting Location

American Redstart
Setophaga ruticilla

Observation Calendar

J F M A M J J A S O N D

Male: Black overall with large orange bands on wings and outer tail feathers; bright red/orange patch on side of chest; belly white; feet and legs black.

Female: Overall olive-grey with large yellow bands on wings and tail; white eye-ring, broken; yellow on sides of white chest; white belly; feet and legs black.

Voice: Song is a series of high-pitched thin notes ending downward. Call is *chip*.

Food: A variety of insects, wild berries and seeds.

Nest/eggs: Compact woven cup built with plant down and grass, lined with weeds, hair and feathers, covered on the outside with lichens, plant down and spider's web, in woodlands and swamps. 4 eggs.

Bay-breasted Warbler

Dendroica castanea

Size Identification

Foot: Anisodactyl

Observation Calendar

J F M A M J J A S O N D

Male: *Spring:* Deep rust patch on top of black head; rust on chin and along sides of chest; grey back with black banding; two white wing bars; wings and tail are black with white edges; belly white with soft rust on sides; rump white; buff patch on either side of neck; feet and legs black with hints of red. *Fall:* head changes to olive/yellow; back is yellow/olive; chest is white with pink on sides, rump is buff.
Female: Duller with less rust on neck and sides.

Egg: Actual Size

Did you know? The quickest way to identify the Bay-breasted Warbler is to locate the buff patch on the side of the neck.

Voice: Difficult to distinguish from other warblers. Song is high pitched *seetsy seetsy seetsy*. Call *see*.
Food: A variety of tree dwelling insects.
Nest/eggs: Loosely woven cup nest built of twigs, dried grass and spider's web, lined with small roots, hair and fine grasses, in tree or shrub, 4-8 metres above ground. 4-7 eggs.

Nesting Location

Blackburnian Warbler
Dendroica fusca

Observation Calendar

J F M A M J J A S O N D

Male: Bright orange-yellow chin, top of head and eyebrow set against black; black band running through eye; back black with white banding; wings and tail black with white edges; large white band on wing; feet and legs red and black; rump white.

Female: Similar to male except orange-yellow is paler; cheeks grey; belly grey.

Voice: Variable song is high-pitched and thin with a mixture of signal chirps and trills, *tsip tsip tsip titi tzeeeeee.*

Food: A variety of insects and berries.

Nest/eggs: Cup nest built with plant down and spider's web, lined with hair, small roots and grass, in tree or shrub, 25 metres above ground. 4-5 eggs.

Blackpoll Warbler

Dendroica striata

Observation Calendar

J F M A M J J A S O N D

Male: *Spring:* Black head with white cheeks; back grey with black banding; wings and tail black with white edges; chin white; chest white with black banding; rump white; two white wing bars; feet and legs black and red. *Fall:* Olive green overall with light banding on sides.

Female: Olive on top with thin black banding; back olive with black banding; wings and tail black with white edges, two white wing bands, chin and chest grey with small specks of black; belly grey.

Voice: High-pitched *zi zi zi zi zi* growing louder. Call is *chip.*
Food: A variety of insects.
Nest/eggs: Bulky cup built with small twigs, grasses, weeds and moss, lined with hair, plant fibres and feathers, in conifer tree or shrub, about 2 metres above ground. 4-5 eggs.

Black-throated Blue Warbler

Dendroica caerulescens

Observation Calendar

J F M A M J J A S O N D

Male: Blue-grey head and back; black face mask with black bill; chest white; wings and tail black with white edges; feet and legs black.

Female: Olive-brown head, back and wings with lighter tone on chin, chest and belly; black bill; thin buff eyebrows; feet and legs black; wings and tail olive-brown with white edges.

They have been seen in Halifax/Dartmouth area and central regions of the province.

Voice: A husky song, "I am soo lazzzzy," and a call that is flat *tip*.

Food: A variety of insects, fruits and seeds taken mainly on ground or low lying branches.

Nest/eggs: Bulky cup of spider's web, dead wood, twigs, leaves and grass, lined with dark rootlets in tree or shrub close to ground. 3-5 eggs.

Black-throated Green Warbler

Dendroica virens

Observation Calendar

J F M A M J J A S O N D

Male: Olive head and back; yellow around eyes and on cheeks; black throat and chest changing to speckled black on white on belly and chest; black banding along sides of belly; wings and tail are black with white edging; two white wing bars feet and legs brown-black; white rump.

Female: Yellow on throat with minimal black.

Voice: Song has a variety of accents, *zee zee zee zuu zee*, and sounds like "sleep sleep little one sleep."

Food: Variety of insects and fruit.

Nest/eggs: Compact cup of fine bark, twigs, grass, lichens and spider's web, lined with hair, fur, feathers and small roots, in tree or shrub, 1-25 metres above ground. 3-5 eggs.

Black-and-white Warbler

Mniotilta varia

Observation Calendar

J F M A M J J A S O N D

Male: Black-and-white striped from crown down entire body length; feet and legs charcoal; bill is thin and black with thin yellow line at mouth opening.

Female: Similar to the male except striping on chest and belly is grey and white, throat is white.

Did you know? The Black and White Warbler is one of the earliest migrants to return to the province in spring.

Voice: Seven or more squeaky calls *weesee, weesee, weesee, weesee, weesee, weesee, weesee.*

Food: A variety of insects, mainly gypsy moths and tent caterpillars.

Nest/eggs: Cup built of leaves, grass, hair and bark, at base of tree or near a boulder. 4-5 eggs.

Canada Warbler

Wilsonia canadensis

Size Identification

Egg: Actual Size

Foot: Anisodactyl

Observation Calendar
J F M A M J J A S O N D

Male: Dark greyish-blue head and back; eyes have white and yellow ring; black under eyes; yellow under chin extends to lower belly with a band of black speckles across chest similar to a necklace; wings and tail black edged in white; feet and legs red; black bill has grey underside, white rump.
Female: Duller overall with black speckled necklace across chest being very faint.

Voice: Richly varied musical song starting with a chip.
Food: A variety of insects including beetles, mosquitoes and larvae of moths and flies.
Nest/eggs: Bulky cup nest built of weeds, bark and leaves, lined with rootlets, plant down and hair, on or near ground in moss-covered area. 3-5 eggs.

Nesting Location

Chestnut-sided Warbler

Dendroica pensylvanica

Observation Calendar

J F M A M J J A S O N D

Male: Bright lemon-yellow crown with chestnut down sides of chest; black band running through eye from black bill; black and white banding on back with yellow tinting; wings and tail black with white edges; feet and legs black; chin and belly white.

Female: Similar to male except mask is duller and chestnut on sides is reduced.

Did you know? Audubon declared these birds as rare but, with the clearing of woodland, sightings have increased.

Voice: A territorial song—*sweet sweet sweet I so sweet.*
Food: A variety of insects including caterpillars, moths and beetles.
Nest/eggs: Loose cup of stems, grass and plant down, lined with grass and hair, in briar tangles, hedges or shrubs, up to 2 metres above ground. 3-5 eggs.

Common Yellowthroat

Geothlypis trichas

Male: Yellow chin, chest and belly contrast with a dark black mask which runs from bill, around eyes to lower neck; white line blends into an olive head, back, wings and tail; feet and legs grey.

Female: Light brown without the distinctive mask.

Voice: A very high—pitched song, *witchity, witchity, witchity,* that is heavily accented.

Food: Caterpillars, beetles, ants and other small insects.

Nest/eggs: Bulky cup of grass, reeds, leaves and moss, lined with grass and hair, on or near ground, in weed stalks or low bushes. 3-5 eggs.

Magnolia Warbler

Dendroica magnolia

Observation Calendar
J F M A M J J A S O N D

Male: Grey head with small eyebrow stripe of white above eye; black mask; yellow chin; chest and belly yellow with black banding; back grey with black banding; wings and tail grey with white edges; two white wing bars; white rump.
Female: Similar to male except banding on chest is narrower; face is grey without black mask and white eyebrow; white eye ring.

Voice: A short melodic song *weeta weeta weeta wee.*
Food: A variety of insects and spiders.
Nest/eggs: Loosely built cup nest of grass, moss and weed stalks, lined with dark roots, in small conifers along the edge of wooded areas and in gardens. 3-5 eggs.

Mourning Warbler

Oporornis philadelphia

Foot: Anisodactyl

Observation Calendar

J F M A M J J A S O N D

Egg: Actual Size

Male: Grey hood with olive back; yellow chest and belly with black collar; bill black with pale underparts; wings and tail dark with yellow edges; rump yellow; feet and legs brown.
Female: Hood is duller; broken white eye ring; wings and tail olive ending in black with white edges; chest pale grey.

Not very common. Seen in northern Cape Breton and confirmed in Minas Basin area.

Voice: Loud ringing *chirry chirry chirry chorry.*
Food: A variety of insects and spiders.
Nest/eggs: Bulky cup of leaves, vines, grass, weeds and bark, lined with fine grasses, rootlets and hair, on or near ground. 3-5 eggs.

Nesting Location

Northern Parula Warbler

Parula americana

Foot: Anisodactyl

Egg: Actual Size

J F M A M J J A S O N D

Male: One of the smallest warblers. Rust colour under chin turning grey at belly and rump; wings and tail feathers black with white edges; small patch of yellow-green on back; legs and feet black; black bill is long and thin; two distinct white bars on wings.

Female: Patch on back is duller and belly is light yellow.

Did you know? Parula means "little titmouse." The movements of the Parula Warbler are very similar to the chickadee and the titmouse.

Voice: Repeated song sounding like a twitter which ends in a *yip*.

Food: A variety of insects

Nest/eggs: Cup of twigs, leaves and moss, hanging in tree branches, 2-30 metres above ground built. 3-7 eggs.

Nesting Location

Northern Waterthrush

Seiurus noveboracensis

Observation Calendar

J F M A M J J A S O N D

Male/Female: Brown head and back with distinctive yellow eyebrow running to back of head; chest pale yellow with dark pronounced banding running down to lower belly; legs pink and red; bill black and pink; short tail.

Concentrations seen in Cape Breton Highlands National Park.

Voice: A ringing song which drops off at the end. Call is a metallic *chink*.

Food: A variety of insects and water bugs, crustaceans, small fish, mollusks.

Nest/eggs: Cup or dome of moss, twigs, bark and leaves, lined with moss, hair and fine grass on ground in upturned roots or fallen trees. 4-5 eggs.

Ovenbird

Seiurus aurocapillas

Observation Calendar

J F M A M J J A S O N D

Male/Female: Olive overall with distinctive mark on head that is orange outlined in black, running from bill to the back of the neck; chest white with black speckles; bill dark on top with yellow on underside; black eyes surrounded by white.

Voice: A progressively louder, *teecher, teecher, teecher, teecher.*
Food: Snails, slugs, worms, spiders and most other insects.
Nest/eggs: Covered bowl, with side entry made of dead leaves, grass, moss and bark, lined with small roots, fibres and hair, on ground in depression. 3-5 eggs.

Palm Warbler
Dendroica palmarum

Foot: Anisodactyl

Egg: Actual Size

Observation Calendar
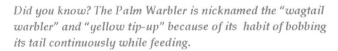
J F M A M J J A S O N D

Male/Female: *Spring:* Rust crown that changes to brown on back of head and back; bright yellow eyebrow; brown cheeks; yellow chin and chest with rust speckles; yellow belly; rump yellow; wings and tail black and brown with white edges; feet and legs black; black bill. *Fall:* Overall browner and duller.

Did you know? The Palm Warbler is nicknamed the "wagtail warbler" and "yellow tip-up" because of its habit of bobbing its tail continuously while feeding.

Seen along the Atlantic shores and the interior of the province.

Voice: Song is *zee zee zee* that rises. Call is sharp *suuup*.
Food: A variety of insects and weed seeds.
Nest/eggs: Nest of dry grass and weed stalks, lined with fine grass, at the base of a tree or shrub. 3-5 eggs.

Nesting Location

Wilson's Warbler
Wilsonia pusilla

Observation Calendar

J F M A M J J A S O N D

Male: Black patch on top of olive-green head; back olive-green; face, cheeks, chin and belly yellow; wings and tail black with white and yellow edges; feet and legs red-pink; short bill, black with red along opening.
Female: Similar to male except the amount of black patch on top varies.

Small pockets of breeding areas around the province including Halifax-Dartmouth, Ecum Secum, and Cape Breton Highlands.

Voice: Song is a short series of *chet chet chet.*
Food: A variety of insects including flying insects and berries.
Nest/eggs: Concealed cup nest built of grass, leaves and some hair, on ground at base of tree. 4-6 eggs.

Yellow Warbler

Dendroica petechia

Observation Calendar

J F M A M J J A S O N D

Male: Yellow throat and chest; olive back; wings and tail black and olive with yellow highlights; chest barred with chestnut strips; bill and feet reddish black.
Female: Similar to male only darker and lacks chestnut markings on front chest.

Voice: A sweet and rapid *tsee, tsee, tsee, tsee, titi-wee.*
Food: Insects with large quantities of caterpillars, beetles and moths. Young birds are fed earthworms as well.
Nest/eggs: Cup of milkweed, hair, down and fine grasses, built in upright fork of tree or bush. 3-6 eggs.

Yellow-rumped Warbler

Dendroica coronata

Observation Calendar
J F M A M J J A S O N D

Male/Female: *Spring:* Yellow rump and yellow patch on either side of chest; yellow crest set against grey head; black mask running from black bill; back grey with black banding; wings and tail black with white edges; two white wing bars; chin white; chest white with black band; feet and legs charcoal; white eyebrow. *Fall:* Similar but duller markers, no black mask, more brown and buff overall.

Did you know? A very abundant warbler that was once called Myrtle Warbler and was thought to be two different species because of its change of plumage.

Voice: Song is light musical notes. Call is *cheeeck.*
Nests: In gardens and conifer forests.
Food: A variety of insects and fruit.
Nest/eggs: Deep cup of twigs, bark, plant down and fibres, lined with hair feather and fine grass, in tree or shrub near trunk. 3-5 eggs.

Cedar Waxwing

Bombycilla cedrorum

Size Identification

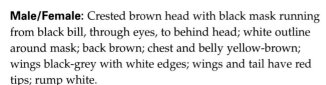
Foot: Anisodactyl

Egg: Actual Size

Observation Calendar
J F M A M J J A S O N D

Male/Female: Crested brown head with black mask running from black bill, through eyes, to behind head; white outline around mask; back brown; chest and belly yellow-brown; wings black-grey with white edges; wings and tail have red tips; rump white.

Did you know? The name derives from the fact that their wings and tail look as though they have been dipped in red wax.

Voice: Extremely high pitched *seeee*.
Food: A variety of berries.
Nest/eggs: Loose woven cup of grass, twigs, cotton fibre and string, lined with small roots, fine grass and down, in open wooded areas in tree or shrub, 2-6 metres above ground. 4-5 eggs.

Nesting Location

Whip-poor-will
Caprimulgus vociferus

Observation Calendar

J F M A M J J A S O N D

Male/Female: Grey fluffy bird with brown cheeks; short black rounded wings; short tail; black bill lightly covered with feathers; large black eyes.

Rarely seen, sometimes heard in the Halifax-Dartmouth area and near Antigonish.

Voice: A series of *whip-poor-will, whip-poor-will* with accent on last word.
Food: Flying insects including moths, beetles and grasshoppers.
Nest/eggs: Depression of dead leaves on the ground formed around eggs. 2 eggs.

American Woodcock

Scolopax minor

Size Identification

Foot: Anisodactyl

Egg: Actual Size

Observation Calendar
J F M A M J J A S O N D

Male/Female: Distinctive long, straight, narrow bill of light brown; large brown eyes set back on the head; overall brown-black back with buff underside; feet and legs pale pink. In flight: Short wings explode with clatter.

Did you know? When courtship is taking place, the males will rise up in the air and circle around as high as 15 metres.

Seen in Cape Breton and in Amherst area.

Voice: A deep *peeeeint* and a tin whistle sounding twitter when in flight.
Food: Earthworms, a variety of insects and insect larvae and seeds.
Nest/eggs: Shallow depression on ground lined with dead leaves and needles, in wooded area. 4 eggs.

Nesting Location

121

Black-backed Woodpecker

Picoides arcticus

Observation Calendar
J F M A M J J A S O N D

Male: Black head with a definite yellow crown on top; back, wings and tail black with occasional bands of white at ends; throat, neck and belly white with speckles; feet and legs grey; black bill is long and thin
Female: Similar to male except no yellow crown on top of head.

Did you know? The Black-backed Woodpecker has a tendency to rip large portions of bark off trees excavating for food.

Uncommon, seen only in Cape Breton Highlands National Park and Kejimkujik National Park.

Voice: Very shrill cries, similar to *kiiiik*. Easiest sound to identify is the pounding on trees either excavating for a nest or foraging for food.
Food: Larvae, wood boring beetles, fruits, nuts and a variety of other insects.
Nest/eggs: Cavity of tree with no added material, .5-5 metres feet above ground. 2-6 eggs.

Downy Woodpecker
Picoides pubescens

Foot: Zygodactyl

Observation Calendar
J F M A M J J A S O N D

Egg: Actual Size

Male: Black crown ends in very bright red spot on back of head; white extends from cheeks to lower belly; wings and tail black with white banding; feet and legs grey.
Female: Similar except without red spot on back of head.

Voice: A bright sounding *peek...peek* which may be followed by a rattling call. Listen for bird pounding on trees looking for insects.
Food: Larvae and other tree-dwelling insects.
Nest/eggs: Cavity of tree with no added material, 1-5 metres above ground. 3-6 eggs.

Backyard Feeder

Hairy Woodpecker
Picoides villosus

Larger than the Downy Woodpecker with only a small red head patch, a longer bill and a louder *peek* and rattle.

Birdhouse Nester

Nesting Location

Northern Flicker

Colaptes auratus

Size Identification

Foot: Zygodactyl

Egg: Actual Size

Backyard Feeder

Birdhouse Nester

Nesting Location

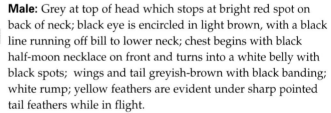

Observation Calendar
J F M A M J J A S O N D

Male: Grey at top of head which stops at bright red spot on back of neck; black eye is encircled in light brown, with a black line running off bill to lower neck; chest begins with black half-moon necklace on front and turns into a white belly with black spots; wings and tail greyish-brown with black banding; white rump; yellow feathers are evident under sharp pointed tail feathers while in flight.

Female: Similar to male except without the black line running from bill.

Voice: Various sounds depending on its use. When claiming its territory a series of *kekekekeke* and when in courtship *woeka-woeka-woeka*.

Food: Digs and pokes on the ground looking for ants and other insects, fruit and seeds. Most of its diet consists of ants.

Nest/eggs: Cavity of tree with no added material, .5-18 metres above ground. 3-10 eggs.

Pileated Woodpecker

Dryocopus pileatus

J F M A M J J A S O N D

Male: Crow-sized woodpecker with a distinctive red crest at top; red band running from black bill to cheek; black extends down neck to tail; cheeks and throat have white banding. In flight, white patches are visible on wings; feet and legs black. **Female:** Black forehead replaces portion of red crest. No red band from bill to cheek.

Did you know? The Pileated Woodpecker can be so aggressive when chiseling away at trees that it can weaken the tree to falling point.

Voice: A quick set of calls, *whucker, whucker, whucker*, in duets sometimes followed by a sharp *kuk* when contacting mate.
Food: Larvae, ants and tree dwelling insects, wild fruits, acorns and beechnuts.
Nest/eggs: Cavity of tree with no added material. 3-4 eggs.

Red-headed Woodpecker

Melanerpes erythrocephalus

Observation Calendar

J F M A M J J A S O N D

Male/Female: Bright red hood over head with grey and black bill; back is black with large distinctive white patches on wings; feet and legs grey; tail feathers are pointed and black; chest and belly white.

Did you know? These woodpeckers are declining because of forestry practices and are competing unsuccessfully with European starlings for nesting locations.

Uncommon, seen near Amherst and in the very southern tip of Nova Scotia.

Voice: Call is a deep hoarse *queer queeeer queeer.*
Food: A variety of insects and insect larvae.
Nest/eggs: Cavity of tree with no added material, 2 -25 metres above ground. 4-7 eggs.

Winter Wren
Troglodytes troglodytes

Observation Calendar
J F M A M J J A S O N D

Male/Female: One of the smallest wrens, with a very short tail; mixed browns on head and back with faint banding in black; wings and tail brown with black banding; feet and legs red; black bill is slightly white on underside; long talons.

Did you know? You may think you are seeing a mouse when you first spot the Winter Wren. They like to keep near the ground and their movements are similar to a field mouse.

Voice: Call is *chip chip* with a variety of songs including twittering and twinkles.
Food: Insects, insect eggs and spiders.
Nest/eggs: Domed cup under roots in tangled growth near ground built with weed, twig, moss, grass and lined with hair and feather. 4-7 eggs .

Index

Alder Flycatcher 33
American Redstart 100
American Tree Sparrow 78

Bald Eagle 27
Bank Swallow 87
Barn Swallow 88
Barred Owl 68
Bay-breasted Warbler 101
Belted Kingfisher 57
Black-and-White Warbler 106
Black-backed Woodpecker 122
Blackbirds 12-16
Blackburnian Warbler 102
Black-capped Chickadee 19
Blackpoll Warbler 103
Black-throated Blue Warbler 104
Black-throated Green Warbler 105
Blue Jay 52
Bobolink 12
Boreal Chickadee 20
Boreal Owl 70
Broad-winged Hawk 44
Brown Creeper 21
Brown-headed Cowbird 13
Bunting 17

Canada Warbler 107
Cardinal 18
Cedar Waxwing 119
Chestnut-sided Warbler 108
Chickadees 19-20
Chimney Swift 91
Chipping Sparrow 79
Cliff Swallow 89
Cooper's Hawk 45
Creeper 21
Crossbills 22-23
Crow 24

Dark-eyed Junco 54
Doves 25-26
Downy Woodpecker 123

Eagles 27
Eastern Kingbird 56
Eastern Meadowlark 62
Eastern Phoebe 74
Eastern Wood-Pewee 72
European Starling 15
Evening Grosbeak 38

Falcons 28-29
Finches 30-32
Flycatchers 33-37

Golden-crowned Kinglet 58
Goldfinch, American 30
Grackle 14
Gray Catbird 94

Gray Jay 53
Gray Partridge 41
Great Crested Flycatcher 34
Great Horned Owl 69
Grosbeaks 38-40
Grouse 41-43

Hairy Woodpecker 123
Harrier 44
Hawks 45-50
Hermit Thrush 95
Horned Lark 60
House Finch 32
House Sparrow 80
Hummingbird 51

Jays 52-53
Junco 54

Kestrel 55
Kingbird 56
Kingfisher 57
Kinglets 58-59

Lapland Longspur 61
Lark 60
Least Flycatcher 35
Lincoln's Sparrow 81
Longspur 61

Magnolia Warbler 110
Marsh Hawk (see Northern Harrier)
Martin 63
Meadowlark 62
Merlin 28
Mourning Dove 25
Mourning Warbler 111

Nighthawk 64
Northern Cardinal 18
Northern Flicker 124
Northern Goshawk 46
Northern Harrier 47
Northern Parula Warbler 112
Northern Saw-whet Owl 70
Northern Shrike 76
Northern Waterthrush 113
Nuthatches 65-66

Olive-sided Flycatcher 36
Osprey 67
Ovenbird 114
Owls 68-71

Palm Warbler 115
Peewee 72
Peregrine Falcon 29
Pheasant 73
Phoebe 74
Pigeons (see Rock Dove)
Pileated Woodpecker 125
Pine Grosbeak 39

Pine Siskin 77
Purple Finch 31
Purple Martin 63

Raven 75
Red Crossbill 22
Red-breasted Nuthatch 65
Red-eyed Vireo 97
Red-headed Woodpecker 126
Red-shouldered Hawk 48
Red-tailed Hawk 49
Red-winged Blackbird 16
Redstart 100
Robin 93
Rock Dove 26
Rose-breasted Grosbeak 40
Rough-legged Hawk 49
Ruby-crowned Kinglet 59
Ruby-throated Hummingbird 51
Ruffed Grouse 42

Savannah Sparrow 82
Scarlet Tanager 92
Sharp-shinned Hawk 50
Short-eared Owl 71
Shrike 76
Siskin 77
Snow Bunting 17
Solitary Vireo 98
Song Sparrow 83
Sparrows 78-86
Spruce Grouse 43
Starling 15
Swainson's Thrush 96
Swallows 87-90
Swamp Sparrow 84
Swift 91

Tanager 92
Thrushes 93-96
Tree Swallow 90

Vesper Sparrow 85
Vireos 97-99

Warblers 100-118
Warbling Vireo 99
Waxwings 119
Whip-poor-will 120
White-breasted Nuthatch 66
White-throated Sparrow 86
White-winged Crossbill 23
Wilson's Warbler 116
Winter Wren 127
Wood Thrush 97
Woodcock 121
Woodpeckers 122-126
Wren 127

Yellow Warbler 117
Yellow-bellied Flycatcher 37
Yellow-rumped Warbler 118
Yellowthroat 109